CLEANER TO CONTROLLER
Volume Two

Further Reminiscences of the GWR at Taunton

by
W.J. Gardner

THE OAKWOOD PRESS

© Oakwood Press 2000

British Library Cataloguing in Publication Data
A Record for this book is available from the British Library
ISBN 0 85361 568 3

Typeset by Oakwood Graphics.
Repro by Ford Graphics, Ringwood, Hants.
Printed by Inkon Printers Ltd, Yateley, Hants.

Title page: 'Castle' class 4-6-0 No. 4037 *The South Wales Borderers* with the 10.40 am ex-Wolverhampton to Penzance express on 23rd September, 1947, passes Bradford-on-Tone bridge, halfway between Taunton and Wellington. *Roger Venning*

Front cover: Ex-GWR Mogul No. 6327 is seen departing Venn Cross with a Barnstaple-Taunton train on 22nd April, 1960. *Colour-Rail*

Rear cover, top: 'Hall' class 4-6-0 No. 6965 *Thirlestaine Hall* passes through Wellington in 1962. *M.J.E. Deane*

Rear cover, bottom: 'Western' class diesel-hydraulic No. D1028 *Western Hussar* stands at Taunton station on 3rd April, 1965. *C.L. Caddy*

Published by The Oakwood Press (Usk), P.O. Box 13, Usk, Mon., NP15 1YS.
E-mail: oakwood-press@dial.pipex.com
Website: www.oakwood-press.dial.pipex.com

Contents

'ROD' class 2-8-0 No. 3019 takes water on the goods loop lines in Taunton East Yard with an up class 'H' goods train (Tavistock Jn-Rogerstone) in January 1947. This locomotive provided Jack with his first experience of main line goods train working.

Roger Venning

Acknowledgements

My personal thanks go to Roger Venning, who kick-started me into having this second volume of my father's railway memories published. The family have decided that all royalties from this volume will be donated to cancer research.

Colin Gardner
Quedgeley
October 2000

The author would like to acknowledge the help from several photographers who have kindly provided photographs to illustrate this second volume of memoirs. Roger Venning and Pursey Short were both active photographers at the time when I was a fireman in Taunton Shed's top link and hence their records are of particular poignancy for me. I am grateful to Clive Bousefield for his permission to reproduce his photograph of the 'Austerity' 2-8-0 at Taunton.

Bob Chudleigh kindly provided additional information about the wartime accident at Creech St Michael and valuable records of locomotives and rosters for the period shortly before the closure of Taunton Shed. Paul Grant again thoroughly checked the text and provided two Appendices.

'King' class 4-6-0 No. 6012 *King Edward VI* departs Taunton with the down 'Cornish Riviera' on 9th March, 1952. Taunton Shed can be seen on the right. *Peter Tunks*

Preface

Jack Gardner was thrilled when his book *Cleaner to Controller* was published in the early Summer of 1994. Such was his modesty that he had seriously doubted that anyone would be interested by his recollections of his footplate career and it took a long time to persuade him to commit his memories to paper. For me assembling the text proved to be a delightful task and both of us were very grateful that The Oakwood Press made such a good job of producing the book.

The reviewers liked what they read and soon Jack found himself renewing his acquaintance with several old colleagues as well as making contact with many new people who wished to learn more from him. Correspondence flowed in from all over the world thanking him for the joy that his book had brought them, some asking for further details on a certain technical point or his experiences of a particular engine.

All of this helped to stir Jack's incredible memory even more and, encouraged by the Oakwood Press, more material began to fall through my letter box for a second volume of *Cleaner to Controller*.

Looking back over the period covered by this book, it seems that although the travelling public and freight customers might only have viewed the railway as a service industry it was the corporate pride demonstrated by most railwaymen that made them into a valued institution. Jack's long apprenticeship ensured that his handling of locomotives was almost intuitive with the safety of all as his over-riding concern. Searing heat, scalding steam, dusty coal, soot and ashes were just part of a day's work for him. In such conditions footplate crews depended upon mutual trust and team work to create and control the power of the steam locomotive. The simple fact that they only got back what they had first put in now seems to wrangle with so many contemporary values. Only after many hours of hard work on a long run with a heavy train would they have the satisfaction of a job well done, a privilege that modern technology now denies many of us. Some would claim that by the time Jack had begun his footplate career the railways had already begun to decline; but thanks to the Great Western publicity machine of the 1930s it is still possible to view this period as a 'golden age'. Certainly World War II and then the Summer Saturdays of the 1950s created levels of rail traffic that have never been exceeded and so Jack's memories recall a period when the railways were at their busiest.

Sadly for his family and his many friends Jack Gardner died in August 1995. Our memories of time spent in his company live on and his written accounts of his railway career will serve as a legacy to future generations.

Simon Bowditch
Frome

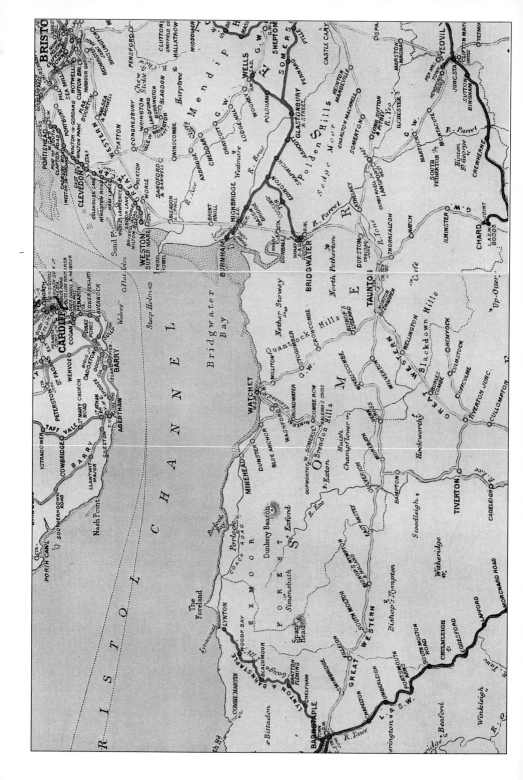

Chapter One

Beam Bridge

From the time of my earliest memories railway engines have been a passion for me. When I was 2, my father, who worked for the GWR, was offered the tenancy of No. 2 Beam Bridge Cottages, situated two miles west of Wellington close to the Somerset and Devon county boundary. This was the second of a row of eight railway cottages built close to the railway embankment, less than a mile from the mouth of Whiteball tunnel. I was sent to school at Sampford Arundel at the age of 3 which entailed a daily walk of half mile in both directions. I was about 4 when I first dared to climb the path used by the permanent way gang to get to the lineside. Here I was dangerously close to the engines as they hurtled down the bank from Whiteball tunnel or pounded up the gradient on the other pair of rails with their heavy loads bound for Exeter, Plymouth and Penzance. On the down trains there was the bonus of seeing the banking engine pushing as hard as it could when assisting the heaviest trains as far as the summit. I must have given many footplate crews palpitations when they saw a small child standing so close to the tracks; later in my life such a sight would have filled me with trepidation.

In addition to this splendid free entertainment most of the steam road vehicles stopped at the roadside at the foot of the steep hill leading to Whiteball, in order to replenish their water tanks from the pool formed by a dammed stream. I saw many vehicles at this spot, the most frequent visitors being W.J. King's Fodens and Sentinels which hauled building stone from the quarries at Westleigh near Burlescombe. The most interesting spectacle would be when Anderton and Rowland's fair passed through and most of the people who lived along the road would watch this entourage climb the hill. All their traction engines would stop and take water before engaging low gear for the mile and a half ascent that lay ahead. The bark of their exhaust could still be heard long after they had disappeared from view. When the road-mending gang were working in the area their steam roller would be a frequent visitor to the pool and while the water lifter was hissing and gurgling away the driver would clean the fire, oil up the valve gear and shaft bearings.

My mother would take us shopping in Wellington on Saturday mornings which meant a two mile walk through Rockwell Green. Sometimes, as a special treat, she would let us ride home on the bus which ran from Wellington as far as Beam Bridge. The bus was an open-topped double-decker and it would stop before it got to the low bridge which carried the railway over the road. Here the conductor would climb the stairs and tell everyone to keep their heads down as we passed under and then it would turn around in the road outside the Beam Bridge Hotel.

In 1926 construction of a new road began which bypassed our village and the narrow twisting road that dropped steeply down from Whiteball. The eastbound road traffic could now speed on its way as far as the sharp bend on the other side of Beam Bridge which then became an accident 'Blackspot'. This remained until the early 1960s when a further road improvement scheme provided a new bridge over the railway line. There used to be a level crossing about 400 yards east of Beam Bridge where the narrow road to Westford and Holywell Lake crossed the railway. This was manned by a Mr Viney who lived in the crossing keeper's cottage nearby. Sometimes on a Sunday or when Mr Viney was on holiday it was my father's duty to man the crossing and my mother and I would walk to the tiny signal cabin and take him his Sunday lunch in a basket.

My father was promoted to Taunton when I was 6 years old and he would cycle the nine miles each way daily in all winds and weathers. My father's two workmates were Dai Jones and Maurice Hext and they frequently visited our home at Beam Bridge on their motorcycles. Dai had a Rover and Maurice had a shining black Sunbeam. On a later visit Dai arrived on a brand new Rudge Whitworth which encouraged my father to acquire a motorcycle for himself and in 1926, having learned to ride, he ordered a Douglas from Locks of Corporation Street, Taunton. This was going to make his commuting to and from work a lot easier and he was looking forward to taking delivery of the machine at the end of August. Then a letter from Taunton Town Council came through the letter box informing him that we had been allocated a council house in Musgrove Road. The order for the bike was cancelled and we moved to Taunton on 13th September, 1926.

'King' class 4-6-0 No. 6018 *King Henry VI* hauls the down 'Torbay Express' on 7th July, 1946. Jack's home as a boy, 2 Beam Bridge Cottages, can just be seen on the left.

Pursey Short

Chapter Two

Cleaning Duties

'51XX' class 2-6-2T No. 5172 made a big impression on my footplate career. On the very first day that I started as an engine cleaner at Taunton Shed, 7th May, 1934, this was the first engine that I cleaned. I was directed to work with a gang of three senior cleaners of whom Joe Hooper and Archie Geyton were firemen who had been put back to cleaning because of the depression in trade. I was to spend 2¾ years as a cleaner and during this period I was to work on this engine many times. We were allowed eight man hours to clean an engine of this size, two hours for each side, two hours for the top and two hours inside the frames which we referred to as 'the gears'. As cleaners we usually worked in pairs so we each had to put in four hours on the task. At the stores you would be issued with a quantity of cotton waste from which you tore off a piece about the size of a ball. This was made into a shape like a bird's nest and then soaked in cleaning oil. At the same time as collecting the cotton waste you would be issued with about four ounces of brick dust which was used to polish the copper rim of the chimney. Having made our way to the stall in which the engine was standing one of us would toss a brass time check and the other would call 'number' or 'blank'. The winner could then choose to clean either the top and right-hand side or 'the gears' and left-hand side.

The area that represented 'the top' was everything above the footplate and 'the gears' everything accessible from underneath in the pit. Before either of us started cleaning we made sure that a red metal 'NOT TO BE MOVED' board was placed on a lamp bracket at the front of the engine. Nobody would move this board except the cleaner who had placed it there. A search would then be made for 'half dirties' which were lightly soiled lumps of cotton waste which would be used to remove the heavy loose grime on the locomotive. Then with a clean lump of cotton waste, soaked in cleaning oil, we would apply a film in a pattern of wavy lines over the paintwork. This was spread all over the particular area you had been allocated by rubbing hard with more clean cotton waste. It was particularly important that the spokes of the wheels were wiped dry and the chargeman cleaner would always check to see that this had been done.

To encourage vigilance among the engine cleaners a reward of 2s. 6d. was given to a cleaner for detecting and reporting broken leaves in the locomotive springs. A similar payment was made for detecting and reporting loose set bolts which secured the taper wedges that kept the big end brasses tight on inside cylindered locomotives. During the time that I spent working on nights I cleaned No. 5172 every other shift. The rest of the night would be spent cleaning an 0-6-0 tank engine which was only allowed six man hours for cleaning. This meant a further three hours each, and to make up the rest of our hours we would be probably be given a further set of 'gears' on another engine. We would divide a set of 'gears' between us by one of us doing the big ends and eccentrics and the other doing the front end and the tops of the motion.

'Star' class 4-6-0 No. 4054 *Princess Charlotte* has just been relieved at Taunton because of a mechanical problem while on an up Kingswear-Paddington express in 1938.
Robert Franklin/Roger Venning Collection

'Star' class No. 4026 stands in the Taunton shed coaling queue, having just hauled the 9.40 am ex-Paddington to Minehead (Saturdays only) express on 28th June, 1947. The train continued its journey to Minehead behind 2-6-2T No. 5172.   *Roger Venning*

Being the most junior cleaner, the week after I started I found myself having to be a 'Call Boy'. On this job we worked three regular shifts, the night turn being 10.00 pm to 6.00 am. The GWR had seen fit to provide each depot with a bicycle for the call boys to go about their work on. This was a very sturdy machine of hefty proportions, built like a tank and painted GWR 'coach brown'. For use after dark it was fitted with a paraffin-burning front lamp which provided no illumination of the road ahead whatsoever. My first night as a call boy was a near disaster as not being sure where some of the drivers lived, I had asked some of the more senior cleaners who had experience of this duty. I was told all sorts of tall stories, including how one driver called Reg Boulter, who lived in Holway, had a trained cat that would jump on you in the dark! Also the quickest way from Palmerston Road to Staplegrove Road was through St Mary's cemetery but watch out for all sorts of ghostly apparitions. As the first call was at Cann Hill and and the second one at Greenway Avenue I decided to take a short cut through Chip Lane and across the railway using Forty Steps footbridge. I soon wished I hadn't because that bike weighed a ton and by the time I had carried it up the steps and down the other side my legs were aching. The next night I went to collect the bike from the stores and found that somebody was playing more tricks on me. The saddle had been bolted up as high as it would go and the wrong way around and the handle bars had been turned around. I left it there and used my own bike and found the whole shift less demanding in physical effort. From then on the call boy's bike stayed in the stores unless I was sent out with a call note during the daytime and I wanted a legitimate reason to spend more time away from the shed. As for Reg Boulter's cat, it didn't exist and I never tried the short cut through the cemetery.

One night a policeman stepped out of the shadows and stopped me wanting to know who I was and what I was doing out at 2.00 am. He was obviously new to his beat and I produced the list of calls I had to make. He realised that I could be an additional pair of eyes and ears for him and asked me to keep a look out for anything untoward that was happening during the hours of darkness, and to let him know. He told me he would be at the same spot each morning at this time. I amused myself thinking up a list of false alarms I could concoct but then considered the possible repercussions for me . I saw him several times during what proved to be a short period for me as call boy, because several newer and younger recruits were taken on and soon I was no longer the junior cleaner.

Although the Great Western publicity department had first published a list of the company's engines and their names as long ago as 1911, with several new and updated editions appearing later, the hobby of train spotting had gathered no great momentum by the mid-1930s. The names and number series given to the various classes of locomotives were still a closed book even to recent recruits to the railway such as myself. Gradually the class names and numbers began to register with me and I was soon able to recognise the similarities between the various types. The named engines that I remember cleaning during this early period included 'Star' class Nos. 4026 *Japanese Monarch*, 4052 *Princess Beatrice*, 4054 *Princess Charlotte*, 4056 *Princess Margaret*, 4072 *Tresco Abbey*, 'Castle' class Nos. 4098 *Kidwelly Castle*, 5003 *Lulworth Castle* and 5077, which was named *Eastnor Castle* when it was first allocated to Taunton Shed in 1938. Other engines

'Bulldog' class 4-4-0 No. 3443 *Chaffinch* is seen on station pilot duties at Taunton on 6th July, 1946.
John Alves

'Bulldog' class No. 3441 *Blackbird* departs Taunton Shed on 4th January, 1947. Ex-Cardiff Railway 0-4-0ST No. 1338 is seen in the distance having just arrived from Bridgwater for its weekly boiler washout.
Roger Venning

included 'Hall' class Nos. 4954 *Plaish Hall*, 4949 *Packwood Hall* and 4953 *Pitchford Hall*, and 'Bulldog' class Nos. 3441 *Blackbird*, 3443 *Chaffinch*, 3444 *Cormorant* and 3453 *Seagull*.

Cleaners at Taunton would only clean the engines allocated to their shed, although we would be detailed to wipe the surplus oil off the motion of the engines working the 'double home' turns from Old Oak Common and Landore Sheds. Some of the engines listed above were probably only allocated to Taunton on a seasonal basis to help out with the additional holiday traffic. At the end of the Summer timetable they would be reallocated by our Divisional Headquarters at Newton Abbot.

As a cleaner I found that I might be directed to clean any engine the chargeman chose and this stage of my career was not spent administering spit and polish only to express passenger engines. Quite frequently I found myself as one of a gang working on humble shunting engines and it was on one of these occasions, when cleaning No. 2127, that I noticed an extra rod running parallel with the one that operated the front sandboxes. I found that this one was fitted to a water cock at the front end of the pannier tanks and the outlet led downwards discharging onto the tyre of the wheel near the leading brake blocks. The operating handle for this cock was situated on the fireman's side in the cab. I often wondered what this arrangement was for and I had to wait until a few years later to find out, when I was booked on a firing turn in Taunton East Yard with a driver named Bill Seaford. We had engine No. 1899 and No. 2127 was working opposite us on the up side shunter. Bill was a nice old gentleman and always encouraged young cleaners to ask questions about engines and all aspects of footplate work. When we stopped for our breakfast break I asked him the purpose of the water feed to the front wheels of No. 2127. He told me that when these engines had been first built at Wolverhampton they had been fitted with wooden brake blocks and that the mechanism was provided to enable water to be dribbled on them to stop them burning during heavy braking. At the time I took this explanation with a pinch of salt because if this were true why didn't the other wheels have this water feed as well? Another possible explanation was that it was used as a flange lubricating device when engines had to venture into tightly curved industrial sidings where flange wear might be a problem.

In later years when I was a fireman on the Chard branch with '58XX' class 0-4-2T No. 5812 I noticed that this engine had a small oil box secured to the main frames just behind the leading wheels. The oil was fed from this container via worsted trimming into a tube which led away to a felt pad which was in contact with the flanges of the leading wheels. No doubt again this modification was intended to reduce wear on the leading wheel flanges.

Not long after when I was fireman on a banking turn at Wellington, I viewed from the footplate an unfamiliar piece of equipment fixed to the left-hand rail of the up main line. I went to investigate and found a cylinder attached to the outer side of the rail. It was about 10 inches long and 10 inches in diameter and had a threaded rod with a nut protruding from the centre of the cylinder. This was attached to another part that went under the rail and upwards to the inside edge of the rail head where, at the level of any passing wheel flange, were three

0-4-2T No. 5812 awaits departure from Taunton with the Chard passenger service on 28th April, 1938.   *John Alves*

Another view of No. 5812. It is seen here on station pilot duties at Forty Steps carriage sidings, on 5th September, 1946. This locomotive gained some notoriety after knocking a hole through the locomotive shed wall.   *Clive Bousfield/Roger Venning Collection*

little spring-loaded plungers; these, when depressed, ejected a small quantity of grease. Obviously the cylinder contained the grease and it was placed at a location where trains would be passing at top speed when descending Whiteball bank. The line beyond this point went into a long right-hand curve towards Taunton so I suppose that this mechanism was provided to minimise flange wear on the left-hand side for the following curve.

Returning to the theme of the details an engine cleaner could notice, I would mention the differences that I found on the special nuts that were used to retain coupling and connecting rods on to their respective crank pins. The large circular nut had two flats for tightening with a special spanner. When these had been tightened they were locked in place by a long bolt part threaded, part tapered which passed through the nut and the crank pin. The difference in this application was that on locomotives where the crankpin was fitted to the wheel boss the bolt was screwed in outwards, so that the head of the locking bolt was towards the centre of the wheel. This seemed logical because if the locking bolt was to become loose it might be held in place by centrifugal force. On the double-framed classes of locomotive such as the 'Bulldogs' and the 'Aberdares' this locking bolt screwed inwards towards the wheel centre. Why this difference was provided I never knew.

During the 1930s we had only had one of the 'Metro' class 2-4-0 tanks at Taunton and this was No. 3582. My intense dislike of this engine began when I was a cleaner and continued when I became a fireman and later as a driver. There wasn't a lot of room for a cleaner to do his work between the big ends and the valve gear, and to make life even more awkward the regulator linkage for the locomotive's 'auto-train' gear passed under the ashpan. To add to the problem No. 3582 was also a 'double bar' engine, i.e. it was fitted with four slide bars to each crosshead, the valves being operated by valve rods which were suspended by a link attached to the motion plate and the leading axle also got in your way. The whole arrangement seemed to have been designed with no thought for ease of access by the cleaner.

The leading axle was supported by a group of four 'volute' springs located above the outside axleboxes and above the running plate beside the smokebox. A 'volute' spring is formed from a flat steel strip wound into a coil. The centre winding of the coil is pushed out about 10 per cent of the diameter. This arrangement prevented easy access to the top of the slide bars and valve gear components, forcing the cleaner to lie on his stomach on the running plate and wriggle his way in with his cotton waste held in front of him in order to clean the 'top motion'.

Later when I was a fireman I counted myself fortunate never to have been called upon to pack the valve spindle glands on this engine. This general lack of convenience was repeated on the footplate. The sandboxes were located about a foot above the level of the bunker shovel plate and you could almost guarantee that with the first shovelful of coal your knuckles would be skinned as they hit the underside of these containers. The whole cab seemed very narrow and to add to the problems the vertical regulator handle was placed high up on the centre of the boiler backhead, out of the reach of the driver or firemen when they were looking over the side of the cab during shunting operations. We had this engine for a while as the west end coach shunter but everyone from the driver to shunter complained so much about its unsuitability for this work that it didn't stay long on this job!

'Metro' class 2-4-0T No. 3582 pauses while on station pilot duties on 11th April, 1939.

John Alves

Another view of No. 3582 at Taunton on 2nd October, 1947. The locomotive had been painted green after a visit to Swindon Works (note the 'SBZ' shedcode). The engine was *en route* to St Blazey, but was retained when it reached Taunton due to the desperate need for a very light locomotive to work in the Engineering Works, 200 yards east of Taunton station, where a petrol mechanical 0-4-0, No. 24, kept breaking down. No. 3582 was also used in Bridgwater Docks when 0-4-0ST No. 1338 was unavailable. Taunton Shed sent an 0-6-0PT, No. 6420, to St Blazey as a replacement. No. 3582 did eventually make it to St Blazey, in July 1948, where it spent its final year. It was the last 'Metro' class locomotive to be withdrawn, in November 1949, having given 50 years of service.

Roger Venning

The turn on which I best remember working with it was the 6.55 am auto working to Hendford Halt on the Yeovil branch. This was a wartime working provided for the Westland Aircraft factory and it called at all the stations and halts along the line. It returned to Taunton propelling the auto-coach with the 7.45 am commuter service and was then used to form the 11.45 am from Taunton to Castle Cary and back. For this sort of work it was a reasonably competent locomotive and despite having only four coupled wheels it could work up a fair turn of speed. Nobody shed any tears when it was eventually replaced by 0-6-0 tank No. 5412.

About the most unpleasant experience I had as a cleaner happened one night in 1935. Working with three other cleaners, we had been set the task of cleaning '49XX' 'Hall' class 4-6-0 No. 4953 *Pitchford Hall*. The engine had worked down to Plymouth and on the return leg it had run into six sheep that had got onto the line near Bradford-on-Tone killing all of them. The driver had reported this to the foreman and he had the shedman hose down the engine's underframes while it was over the servicing pit. I had the job of going underneath to clean 'the gears'. While I was underneath with only a flare lamp to light my way I looked forward and saw a sheep's head staring at me from where it had come to rest on top the vacuum brake cylinder. I came out from under the engine in double quick time and refused point blank to go back to finish the task. Fortunately the chargeman cleaner was sympathetic towards me and put me on cleaning another engine.

Thinking back and considering the jobs that I saw being done often in unreasonable and unsafe conditions just to achieve high availability figures, makes me appreciate the high level of dedication shown by these railwaymen. I saw fitters risk being scalded when replacing a blown joint in the delivery pipe between an injector and a leaking clack valve. With steam still blowing from the pipe this team of skilled men fitted a new flange joint on the delivery side of the injector. To have done the job by the book would have meant the fire being thrown out, the boiler being blown down to empty and then being allowed to cool before starting the job.

Harry Lever was one of the most corpulent boilersmiths I have ever seen and to watch him getting through the firehole was somewhat amusing as he poked and pressed at his huge stomach when easing himself inside a firebox. Once inside he would replace a broken stay, expand a leaking tube or repair a damaged brick arch. Often he would be inside a firebox when there was still 60 lb. per square inch of steam still registering on the gauge with the temperature in excess of 50 degrees Celsius. It was amazing that Harry stayed so corpulent because when he had completed the job he emerged from the firebox perspiring pints of fluid. Such was the devotion to duty shown by the staff in all grades at Taunton Shed during this period.

Not all of the old drivers we had at this time would be willing to engage in conversation with the young cleaners as they liked to maintain their air of seniority, but a few would afford us some insights into their own railway careers and the lessons they had learned. Sidney Oliver Cook remembered his days as the regular fireman on one of the early pioneers of Churchward's 2-cylinder 'Saint' class, No. 2971 4-6-0 *Albion*, when it was a Taunton engine in the early 1920s. He still talked about the engine with great affection referring to it in conversation as 'my *Albion*'. If *Albion* went away on a turn and didn't return on its booked working, Sidney Cook would take this very personally and would send telegrams all over the system 'Return ALBION to Taunton', most frequently offering the excuse that it was due for washing out. Sidney Cook and his *Albion* were almost legendary at Taunton. These had been the days of stringent economy when the foreman would have the coal on the emergency coal stack whitewashed to make sure that not a single lump was taken without his authority.

Like most locomotive depots, Taunton had a Mutual Improvement Class. The purpose of this voluntarily organisation, run by the senior drivers, was to improve the knowledge of aspiring firemen so that they might pass the examinations set by the headquarters inspectors at Swindon and become passed firemen and subsequently drivers. The senior drivers who acted as tutors received no additional pay or official recognition for the valuable task they performed. The classes were usually held between 11 am and 1.00 pm on Sundays, during which time they would expound on aspects of the Rule Book and the finer details of the steam locomotive drawing on the knowledge accumulated in their long railway careers.

As a cleaner who was keen to be promoted to fireman I had to ask for permission to attend these classes from one of the senior drivers, namely Mr W.J. King. This permission was quickly granted and I began to understand the function of each part of the valve gear. Now as I wiped the mess off the connecting rods, eccentric rods, big ends and eccentrics, my menial work began to take on greater importance. The mysteries of the expansion link (or quadrant link as some of the older men used to call it) were lucidly explained and I began to understand how the steam might be made to work expansively in the locomotive's cylinders. I also began to learn remedies for mechanical failures

Un-named 'Hall' class 4-6-0 No. 6958 leaves Taunton's platform 7 with the 11.35 am stopping train to Bristol on 10th January, 1947. The Signal Department is in the background. The Mutual Improvement Classes which Jack attended were held in a room below the water tank.
Roger Venning

which a fireman should be capable of dealing with. Take, for instance, the case of what to do if a spring hanger bolt was broken and needed to be replaced. The axlebox would need to be lifted out of its normal working position by packing an adjacent axlebox between the top of the box and mainframe. Then the wheel of that axlebox would be run up over the head of the coal pick which would be placed on the rail. The axlebox with the broken spring hanger bolt would then be packed between the axlebox and the frame, using a wooden key that could be knocked out of any nearby rail chair. Then run the engine wheel down off the coal pick, remove the packing from the good axlebox, and the engine could then be permitted to proceed with caution to shed where a more permanent remedy would be available.

The Rule Book and General Appendix would be interpreted for us so that we were able to understand why the rules were needed. The details pertaining to 'Wrong Line Orders' included information that every footplateman needed to be conversant with, particularly as one of these might be used if his engine became a failure and an assisting engine was required.

The effectiveness of this voluntary organisation was never officially recognised. When the railways were nationalized in 1948 the new British Transport Commission gave some support to the tutors by providing courses for them at the Staff Training College at Faverdale Hall near Darlington. The purpose of these courses was to improve the presentation and delivery skills of the tutors but, apart from this support, no change was made to the old system

The implementation of the 1955 Modernisation Plan saw the introduction of diesel traction from about 1958 onwards. It was realised with this new form of motive power that a completely new set of skills would be needed by drivers. Accordingly a band of senior drivers was selected and sent on various courses where they learned how to drive the new diesel-hydraulic locomotives, and also how to remedy certain failures that might occur when in service. Six were appointed at Taunton and they took up duties on diagrams due to be worked by diesel locomotives. Acting as tutors to the remaining footplate staff, they eventually ensured that all the Taunton crews became proficient in the driving of the various types of diesel locomotive that worked in our area.

In 1936 I received my first free pass so I decided to use it to travel to Blidworth in Nottinghamshire to spend a holiday with an aunt of mine. My free ticket only took me as far as Birmingham (Snow Hill), from where I had to walk to Birmingham (New Street), and buy privilege rate ticket from there to Nottingham. I had a three hour wait at Bristol (Temple Meads) before I could catch a train to Birmingham via Cheltenham and Honeybourne. Here I saw LMS 'Jubilee' class 4-6-0 No. 5552 *Silver Jubilee*, at that time still resplendent in shiny black paint and chromium plate work. I also remember seeing 'Grange' class No. 6805 *Broughton Grange*. My train from Birmingham went via Derby where I had to change for Nottingham. The locomotive on this service was of particular interest because it was a Stanier 2-6-4T, No. 2537. Its modern appearance was a marked contrast to the Dean Standard Goods engine carrying the same number which we had at Taunton Shed.

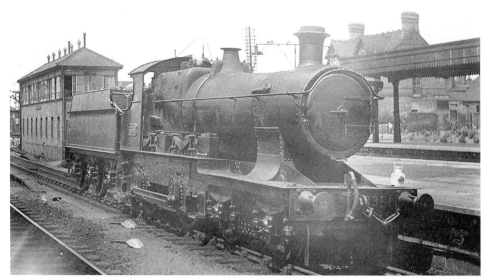

Un-named 'Bulldog' class 4-4-0 No. 3361 is seen on station pilot duties at Taunton in the late 1930s.   *Robert Franklin/John Alves Collection*

'3150' class 2-6-2T No. 3184 performs West End station pilot duties in the late 1930s.
Robert Franklin/John Alves Collection

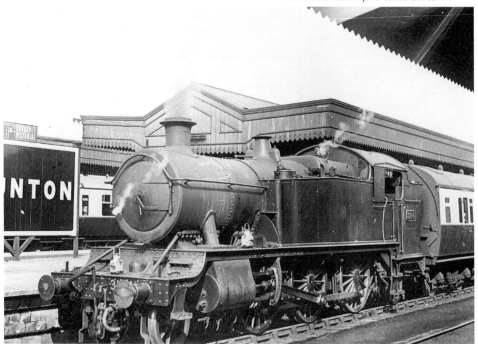

Chapter Three

Promotion to Fireman

Great Western fireman were favoured by not being required to clean the fireboxes of their locomotives before they disposed of their engine. On arriving back at shed a team of men in the form of firedroppers, coalmen, tube cleaners, boiler washers and general shed labourers took care of all these duties.

The work of the firedropper was particularly unpleasant as he had to shovel out all the residual fire and accumulations of clinker that adhered to the firebars. He was aided in his work by a special shovel made up from an old fireman's shovel with a long piece of a former boiler tube as a handle. He used this to ladle out all the ash and clinker from the firebox into the fire pit. The handle of the firedropper's shovel would become burnished by the action of it passing through his hands as it slid in and out of the firebox. Needless to say most firedroppers' hands were like leather after only a few weeks on this job.

On the front left-hand side of the larger locomotive tenders was located the hand brake, the water valve for the left-hand injector and an air cock. This device could be opened to admit air to the reservoir of the vacuum brake which, if necessary, would release the brake on the tender. On the right-hand side of the tender was the water scoop handle, the water valve for the right-hand injector and an emergency air cock which admitted air to the vacuum brake train pipe behind the connections of the tender to the engine. This was an emergency brake application valve which could be used in the event of a blockage in the flexible connections between the engine and the tender. Ice could block the flow of air in the pipe and it was a fact that all enginemen had to keep in mind, particularly in cold weather.

Firemen who worked on the larger passenger engines always liked to carry a spare shovel which they would wedge down behind the emergency air valve. Sometimes a firedropper would find a brand new shovel stowed in this location which he would convert for his own use. The wooden shaft and handle was of no use to him and so he would throw it overboard and quickly cover it in hot ashes which would burn out all the wood work. This left him with a nice new blade to fit to his own polished steel handle. The blade of a firedropper's shovel did not have a very long life in the arduous work of shovelling hot ashes and clinker out of a locomotive firebox. Management took a very dim view of the wanton destruction of equipment to make firedroppers' shovels. However, as an effective piece of equipment it had no equal in the hands of an experienced man and it ensured the rapid movement of engines through the servicing area. This fact was much appreciated by the foreman who tolerated their misdemeanours.

The firedroppers were also responsible for clearing out the ashpans and smokeboxes, the fine char obtained from this end of the boiler was kept separate from the rough ashes thrown out of the firebox. The firedropping shovel found on the fire iron tool rack of the tender was useless for the rapid removal of fire and clinker from a firebox. As such firedroppers always guarded the 'special tool' of their trade very carefully.

'2721' class 0-6-0PT No. 2748 and its shunter's truck in Taunton West Yard while acting as yard pilot on 5th May, 1938.   *John Alves*

'Dean Goods' class 0-6-0 No. 2472 has just arrived at Taunton's platform 7 on a Summer Saturday in 1939. The train appears to be a Minehead-Paddington through train. A Taunton 4-6-0 locomotive would probably have taken over from here.   *John Alves*

In the late 1930s the west end of Taunton station was a very busy place and the west end coach shunter was a busy shift to work. The early turn signed on at 5.15 am to come off shed at 6.00 am and the engine provided for this work was usually one of Taunton's surviving Dean Standard Goods 0-6-0 tender engines, either No. 2527, 2537 or 2578. During the weekends of the summer months engine cleaners would find themselves booked out as firemen. The most senior of the engine cleaners would take the earliest turn available and so if there was only one firing job going , possibly the 9.45 pm up side freight shunter, this individual might find his working week looking like this:

Monday to Friday: Engine Cleaning, 6.00 am to 2.30 pm
Saturday: Up side Freight Shunter 9.45 pm

From this you can see that flexible rostering is not a new idea as we were working under these arrangements in the 1930s.

By 1935 the management decided that the electrically-operated turntable at Taunton Shed should be removed and replaced by a hand-operated one. While this work was being carried out there were substantial alterations to engine rosters and additional space had to be made to accommodate engines in the adjacent carriage sidings. The breakdown vans were also stabled in those sidings at this time and the opportunity was taken to lengthen the servicing pits on the incoming and outgoing roads. The shallow pit on the outgoing road was deepened at this time which did not meet with the approval of some of the shorter drivers who found that they could no longer reach the crank axle to fill the bearing oil reservoirs during preparation. A couple of wooden stools were provided for their convenience and an additional water column was added just outside the shed exit which enabled engines to be watered on either the incoming or the outgoing road.

Engine cleaners were not at this time issued with caps and had to wait until they were promoted to the rank of fireman before they received one. Firemen and drivers received an annual clothes issue and this was the time when the cleaners would try to scrounge a second-hand cap from one of their senior colleagues. Some sort of headgear was really essential when you considered the filthy nature of the work we were expected to do. During the period that the turntable was out of use I was given a firing turn on an engine that was sent to Exeter for turning. As a temporarily upgraded fireman I was paired with Percy Pope on this light engine run with a '49XX' 'Hall' class. The engine was out in the carriage sidings but once we had prepared it we wasted no time in travelling to Exeter, turning it , and getting home again. I am not sure if Percy had been offered an early finish but we were certainly not hanging about on this return journey and I was enjoying the run, particularly as I didn't have a lot of shovelling to do. I had been cleaning all night before this trip came up and my head started to nod as we passed Hele and Bradninch. Here the wind caught my cap and was blown away into the dark morning, never to be seen again.

We went to Exeter and back in just over an hour and a half, but to have this credited to me as a firing turn and to be paid at the higher rate the rules said that I had to be on duty in that role for at least two hours. So here I was back cleaning engines again, no firing turn credited to me, no extra money and minus my cap! At that time we had to do 313 firing turns before we qualified for the first year fireman's rate of pay of 9s. 6d. per day. The magic figure of 313 was the number of working days in one year.

During the summer of 1935 two Taunton footplatemen found themselves on the carpet over an incident that occurred on the Minehead line. Driver Bill Coward and firemen Bill Curtis were working an afternoon train down to Minehead. They were rolling down the 1 in 92 gradient over Leigh Wood level crossing and the distant signal for Leigh Bridge crossing was clear. It was only then that fireman Curtis realised that Leigh Bridge signal box must be switched in and that he should change the staff. Realising that he did not have the token ready in the Whittaker token exchanger on the side of the engine, he slid the exchanger out to collect the token for the next section (Leigh Bridge-Williton) and just dropped the token for the previous section (Crowcombe-Leigh Bridge) over the side close to the tablet catcher, hoping it would be retrieved from the ballast by the signalman. When the train arrived at Williton station fireman Curtis claimed that there had been a malfunction of the Whittaker apparatus at Leigh Bridge and the token had been knocked to the ground. But a passenger had reported what had happened which resulted in both Curtis and Coward being reprimanded. The dropped token had been lost incurring long delays all along the line, until the lineman put the instrument right by withdrawing another token. The lost token was found, three weeks later resting on the top of a coach bogie at Swansea!

In the winter of 1935 I had hoped to go to a party on Christmas Eve which fell on a Tuesday, but when I looked at the duty sheet on the Monday I saw that I was booked out to fire to a passed fireman named Bill Bond. The shift began at 6.30 pm and involved a specially extended period of work with the west end carriage shunter, which would have to cope with the need to have all the incoming stock stabled in the correct position for their next working on Christmas Day, Boxing Day or the 27th December. We signed on and walked to the west end of the station and found that we had a Collett '2251' class 0-6-0 tender engine, No. 2268, for this turn. This was an added bonus because these had a wider and thus more comfortable cab than the Dean Goods engines and it was also easier to observe the shunter's signals from the footplate of these engines. We started by assembling vehicles for the 11.20 pm Swindon parcels. Then at about 9.00 pm a series of trains arrived resulting in us collecting five coaches off the Exeter service, three off the Barnstaple and a further four from the Minehead service. It was official policy to avoid making any unnecessary movements but the 12 coaches assembled behind the engine represented quite an awkward load to be split up. The last four of these were now to be shunted to the Minehead departure bay and so we set off from No. 7 up relief platform, crossing the the up main, down main and then out onto the down relief and drew forward to stop under Taunton West Junction's home signal. We then received the sign to set back from the shunter who was riding in the last coach when he waved his white handlamp from side to side. I told Bert that I had seen the shunter's signal and so he began to move the engine backwards, propelling the coaching stock to the Minehead bay. We had only travelled about five coach lengths when I lost sight of the shunter's lamp because of the curve of the line. I told Bert who applied the brake and we slowed right down. This was evidently not slowly enough because as we were passing under the signal gantry which carried West Station signal box's down starters we stopped with a sudden lurch.

Our shunter came forward and said we had damaged the stop blocks at the end of the Minehead bay platform. He then cut-off what coaches he could and we disposed of them in the carriage sidings. After some more shunting movements we went back over to the up side again and dealt with the London Parcels and various other trains over the next hour or so. By 10.30 pm we were standing under Forty Steps bridge waiting for a further shunt when a passenger train stopped at Taunton West Station up relief home signal. A window opened in the coach alongside our footplate and two girls called out 'Merry Christmas!' I said 'Thank you', but Bert was brooding over the possible consequences of our rough shunt and muttered something about it being a right bloody Christmas so far.

Early in the following January we had to attend an inquiry into the incident where Bert accepted responsibility, admitting that he should have been more cautious considering that we were shunting 12 coaches. He was let off with a caution. The stop blocks at the end of the Minehead departure bay were replaced with a large solid concrete structure which remains there to this day.

As my seniority among the cleaners rose I found that I was booked to an increasing number of firing turns. However, when the summer rush was over these came few and far between. It was then back to engine cleaning and it was about this time in 1936 that I had a brush with one of the more crusty and unapproachable senior drivers in Taunton's No. 1 Passenger Link. Even at this late date drivers of Tom Penny's seniority could count upon having their own engine for the more prestigous turns allocated to Taunton. At this time Tom's engine was 'Star' class 4-6-0 No. 4052 *Princess Beatrice*, and it was the job of the senior engine cleaner on night shift to clean the engine for the 7.50 am Taunton to Paddington service which ran via Bristol. This was a 'double-home' turn with Tom and his fireman working through to Paddington on Mondays, Wednesdays and Friday, booking off at Old Oak Common and working back to Taunton on the following day. The crew for this turn signed on at 6.20 am and were allowed 1¼ hours' preparation time for a 4-cylinder 4-6-0 engine and had to be ready to leave shed to go to the station at 7.35 am.

Despite the prestige attached to this working crews always 'niggled' about it because, being 163 miles from Taunton to Paddington via Bristol, under the mileage payment agreement then in force they received 10 hours pay for the turn. They always claimed they should have received more because they were required to prepare the engine at Taunton and dispose of it at Old Oak Common, resulting in them being on duty for more than 10 hours. As one of the two senior cleaners on night shift on this occasion it fell to me to clean the top part of the valve motion to the rear of the smokebox. The drill for this awkward task was to clean all the running board and then lie down and reach full length under the boiler, wipe off the valve gear and the large cast motion plate that held it in position. Below this position was the casting that held the bogie pivot pin which was always filled and sometimes overflowing with dirty oil. We used all the old cotton waste to mop up this mess and we smeared this oil all over the smokebox, ensuring that the glistening black smokebox and chimney contrasted nicely with the highly burnished copper cap of the chimney.

The whole task took us most of the night shift as cleaning an engine and tender such as this one would take the full allowance of 14 man hours. We worked hard all through the night and on Monday morning she looked a treat. Tom Penny said nothing to us when he came to prepare the engine but on the following Wednesday morning he was in a foul frame of mind. He went over to the head foreman, Mr James, and complained that his engine had not been cleaned properly, referring specifically to the top motion work.

Mr James sent for Ned Widgery, the chargeman cleaner and tore him off a strip and then in his turn Ned, now furious, came to us where we were just finishing off the footplating. On checking the cleanliness of the engine for himself he pronounced himself satisfied with our efforts and he then called Mr James over to inspect it for himself and he too could find nothing to complain about. Mr James then told Tom Penny that he was wrong, leaving Tom to wriggle out of his predicament by saying that he was complaining about yesterday when he had prepared the engine at Old Oak Common before working home. The upshot of this was that next time Tom was at Old Oak Common he went around the corner to Lyons Chocolate Factory and bought us each a big bag of sweets which he presented with an apology for the misunderstanding he had created! Old Oak Common never cleaned other depot's engines and did remarkably little to their own.

Both Mr James, who was head foreman at Taunton when I started, and his successor, Mr Reg Aston, were most fastidious about the regularity of boiler washing of Taunton-based engines. There was a weekly rota which was strictly adhered to and this helped ensure minimum repair costs and prevented incidents of priming or foaming when the engines were working. With the regularity of this procedure and the good quality of Taunton's water it was not surprising that the boilers of Taunton engines enjoyed a long and productive life. I suspect that the Severn Valley Railway came to appreciate this fact when they restored 'Hall' class 4-6-0 No. 4930 *Hagley Hall* from scrapyard condition as this had been a Taunton engine in the late 1950s and early 1960s.

During an afternoon shift in 1936 I found myself firing to a passed fireman called Charlie Brown. We were supposed to have worked the 12.30 pm Wellington banker but in order to make up the full eight hours our booked working was altered so that we would work the 4.50 pm Taunton to Exeter passenger train, the return working of which would see us signing off duty at about 7.45 pm. On the day, however, it was decided that as we were only passed cleaner and passed fireman the No. 2 Link men would work to Exeter and back as far as Wellington where we would relieve them to effect our return to Taunton. We advised the signalman about this arrangement and soon after 7.00 pm we had our banking engine brought over to the siding off the up platform in order to minimise the walking distance when the changeover was made. We were waiting on the platform for the train which drew in behind 'Star' class 4-6-0 No. 4072 *Tresco Abbey*. On climbing up on the footplate I remarked that the fire was very low but the fireman I was relieving said that the engine was going to shed at Taunton. My driver then reminded him that this engine was scheduled to work the 7.40 pm. Taunton to Bristol service and so I had to get stuck in and rebuild the fire. This work was doubly hard because the front end of the tender was now short of coal and I had to go back into the tender for every shovel I fired. By the time I got to Taunton I had about half a box and I stayed on the footplate to pull forward as much coal as I could for my relief.

Tresco Abbey was then shedded at Taunton and during my period as a cleaner I cleaned this engine, No. 4016 *Knight of the Golden Fleece* and also No. 4098 *Kidwelly Castle*. As a fireman several years later I was surprised to find that I had just climbed aboard 'Castle' class No. 5092 *Tresco Abbey*, the original 'Star' class locomotive having been rebuilt in this form at Swindon in 1938. I wonder how many fireman can claim to have fired this engine in both its incarnations?

As a passed cleaner it was quite common to find that you had been paired for a firing turn with a passed fireman. One of the more entertaining passed firemen was Frank Oaten. He had risen to be of sufficient seniority in his link to be working in the 'double-home' turn to Swansea on Mondays, Wednesdays and Fridays, lodging there overnight and returning the next day. When paired with him I was keen to learn more of main line footplate work and our conversation soon got around to the prestige Swansea job and I asked him what it was like working through the Severn tunnel. He gave me an immediate answer which caught me completely off guard. 'Oh it's not too bad in daylight but it's a sod after dark!' In my naivity I wasted quite a few minutes considering this reply before I realised I was having my leg pulled.

An alternative to working with a passed fireman was to be booked out on the east end coach shunter with one the senior drivers who was on light duties for convalescence purposes. The majority of these men were jealous at the conditions of service we young firemen were then enjoying compared with the tyranny that they had had to put up with. Some of them painted a pretty grim picture of what they had to endure from some of the old men that they worked for back before World War I. These were the days when a driver had his own regular engine and was paid a bonus for saving coal and oil. To make sure that nobody touched the coal in the bunker of his engine between signing off and booking on the next day, the driver would send the fireman to scrounge a bucket of whitewash to brush all over the coal. The driver would go to the Carriage and Wagon Department's store and scrounge a couple of pints of oil which he would use to lubricate the motion of his engine to avoid signing for the oil from the Loco. Department where it would be booked against his engine. One of these old characters, who witnessed me spilling coal, told me how his driver was a maniac for saving coal and would go berserk if he allowed a lump of coal as small as a golf ball to roll over the side of the footplate. To make matters worse he would work the engine so lightly, with the regulator barely open and very short cut-off, that maintaining a bright fire was nearly impossible. The driver also totally forbade him to touch the blower and he found that life was being made completely impossible for him. One of the other fireman suggested that he should put a 'Jimmy' in the blastpipe. This consisted of a piece of ¼ inch iron plate fashioned by the blacksmith which could

GWR Mogul No. 4337 waits in Victory Siding (near Norton Fitzwarren) for the main line to clear on 8th July, 1946. This locomotive will later work as a Wellington banker. *Roger Venning*

2-6-2T No. 4113 is seen at Fairwater Yard, Taunton on 18th January, 1947. It will take a pick-up goods train to Wellington, then spend some hours as a banking engine, before returning to Taunton on another goods train. *Roger Venning*

be dropped edgeways into the blastpipe to spread the blast to fill the chimney. He said that this worked a treat and he used it all the time that he was paired with this particular driver without his knowledge, putting it into position while preparing the engine and removing it during disposal at the end of the shift. This was before the advent of the GWR jumper ring which was fitted to the top of the blastpipe.

Years later when I was having my first look over one of the US Transportation Corps 'S160' 2-8-0s that we used for a short time during World War II, I noticed that the blast nozzle on these had two short steel rods about ⅜ in. diameter welded in a 'X' across the top of the blast nozzle, reminding me of the tale of the 'Jimmy'. Obviously this was to spread the blast so that it filled the chimney and thus improve the steaming capacity of the boiler.

Reverting to the subject of this old driver, I was told that he never missed an opportunity to steal fuel from a coal wagon that was marshalled next to the engine on a freight train. He would be in the wagon throwing lumps of coal back into his bunker at every opportunity.

No steam was ever allowed to go to waste in the atmosphere and many of the old drivers would carry a small coil of asbestos string with which they would repack the spindles of any of the steam valves which might be leaking in the cab. They also insisted that the fireman use the handbrake to stop the engine because they considered that the steam brake wasted more steam than any other fitting on the engine.

Another duty on which a passed fireman might acquire a number of firing turns was on the Wellington banking engine when the Summer service was at its peak. This was a lot more interesting than shunting and I later worked in this link on a regular basis when I was promoted fireman.

A fireman of my own age named Raymond had joined the GWR at Taunton a few months after I started. He was well educated and a physical fitness enthusiast who had recently entered the mile event at the annual Police Sports and had won with a time of 4 minutes 44 seconds. Unfortunately the irregular hours of his new footplate career played havoc with his training schedule and his running performance suffered. He was a very keen field sportsman as well, and it was a pleasure to enjoy an afternoon's shooting with him on a farm near Bradford-on-Tone where he rented the shooting rights. Usually I came home with a rabbit or two which delighted my mother. Having let his athletics training lapse, he kept fit by doing a bit of boxing which he practised in his own personal gym. He encouraged me to visit him and do a bit of 'sparring' with him but I wasn't at all keen on the idea of boxing. However, one day he insisted that I put on a pair of gloves and have a few rounds with him. He was keen to explain the finer points of attack and defence to me and we were soon slinging a few light punches at each other. In the middle of this I thought that I would be clever and drew back my right hand but pushed forward on my left. Ray walked right into this and he was so surprised to have been caught off guard that he let fly and pasted me all around the room. All I could do was cover up. Afterwards he admitted that he had been taken by surprise and said that I should have followed up my temporary advantage, but I had had enough and my arms were sore for days after.

GWR Mogul No. 6364 is seen on the locomotive siding, alongside Taunton Shed, on 11th April, 1939.   *John Alves*

Prairie tank No. 4117 takes water prior to departure from Taunton with an Exeter-bound passenger train, 11th April, 1939.   *John Alves*

Another young fireman was a talented artist by the name of John Dew. If he was sitting in the cabin awaiting orders he would take the blank page from the back of an old notice and start to draw a pencil portrait of anyone who was in the room with him. Nobody took much notice of the way he passed his time until one day he drew a portrait of Archie Gayton and three days later poor Archie died. A few weeks later he drew a portrait of old Joe Hooper and within a week he was dead also. After that if anyone found John in the cabin they wouldn't go in, afraid that he might draw a portrait of them and tempt providence.

Another young fireman was Roger Watson. He was a rather serious young man, not given to levity or jovial conversation. Years later I learned that he was a nationally recognised expert on growing cacti!

Such was the wide range of talent and ability that you could find among the footplatemen at Taunton. When we weren't on duty cleaning engines we enjoyed a good social life and if I wasn't working on a Sunday I would stroll around the town with my mates 'chatting up' the girls. With Taunton being a rural town with not many well paid jobs for young lads of 17 or 18, news got around among the girls that you were an engine cleaner with the prospect of a lifetime of well paid continuous employment ahead of you. Even with your foot on the bottom rung of the career ladder you had a certain status and the girls regarded us as very eligible boyfriends. We knew loads of girls, some of whom were the sisters of other engine cleaners and others who were the daughters of drivers. The year 1936 came and went but then on 9th February, 1937, Frank Penny and myself were each handed a letter and a train ticket. The letter read as follows:

On Monday 15th February you will travel by the 11.08 train to Pontypool Road and present yourself to the Head Foreman Loco. Shed for instruction. As from thenceforward you will consider Pontypool Road as your home depot.

There were no 'ifs' or 'buts', there it was, pack your bag and go and this is what we did. Our train drew into the large island platform at Pontypool Road at about 1.30 pm and just glancing around I realised that there must be an important freight yard here. In fact I was later to learn that there were seven yards, Birkenhead Sidings, South Sidings, Loop Sidings, Old Yard, Coedygric Sidings, New Sidings and North End. The large platform at which we had arrived had a bay at the north end from which the auto-train to Monmouth and Ross ran. There were six tracks through the station; besides the up and down roads on either side of the platform there was another track for freight on the east side and three more tracks on the west side, the outer two of which went via a double junction at the south end where the two sets of tracks disappeared heading westward up a distant valley.

Trying to take all this in we headed for the loco shed where we were directed to the head foreman's office. Here we were joined by another new fireman, Len Western from Weston-super-Mare, who had suffered the same fate as us to be promoted to fireman at Pontypool Road. The foreman welcomed us and introduced us to his chief clerk who gave us our duties for the rest of that week and told us that on the following week we would have a regular shift on one of the shunting engines in the yards. Frank Penny would go to the South Sidings and I was to go to the New Sidings. We were on early turn for the first week and early turn the following week and so this precluded any opportunity of getting home for the weekend because it was impossible to get back to Pontypool Road in time for a 5.00 am start on Monday. Neither of us were married men so we were not permitted any 'visiting home passes' and if we contemplated going home for a weekend we had to buy a privilege ticket costing 5s. 6d. Reading the back of one of these tickets during the course of a journey home I noticed that the fine print stated that the price of this ticket included one shilling, being the full fare through the Severn tunnel.

The shed foreman had arranged lodgings for us with Mrs Watkiss at No. 1 The Walk, New Inn, and she looked after us very well during our stay. She was a widow, aged about 45 with three children. Her husband had been killed in an accident about two years earlier and now she took in lodgers to supplement her income. She charged £1 per week and worked very hard for it. I paid her 2s. 6d. extra per week to do my laundry for me. Finding out that I wouldn't be able to get home for the weekend I wrote to my mother to give her my new address and reassure her that I had found good lodgings. It was my birthday on the following Thursday and when Mrs Watkiss saw a birthday card arrive for me through the post she baked me a cake.

When Saturday came Frank shot off back to Taunton, desperate to see his new girlfriend, leaving me at No. 1 The Walk for the rest of the weekend. He only just managed to get back in time for work on Monday morning by taking the last train to Bristol on Sunday night, then on to Newport were he begged a lift on the 'Up Mail' to Pontypool Road, arriving about 4.00 am.

After lunch on Sunday a nice looking girl, about 18 years old, came to see Mrs Watkiss. I found myself being introduced to Clarris Greenwood-Cox, the daughter of a friend who lived at the other end of the terrace. She was in service in a doctor's house in Clevedon and was home for the weekend. She had an elder sister who was also in service at another house with a different family in the same town. Clarris stayed for tea and we all engaged in polite conversation afterwards, there being no television in those days. For some reason my recent birthday came up in the general chatter and Mrs Watkiss said to Clarris, 'Give Jack a kiss for his birthday!' Quite willingly, came over to me, sat on my knee, put her arms around my neck and gave me a long kiss on the mouth. 'Wow', I thought, 'That was nice' and on the strength of this I asked if she would like to go to the cinema with me the following night. She said that she was supposed to go back to Clevedon in the morning but something was cooked up with her sister to give a message to her boss that she was unwell and wouldn't be back until Thursday. I didn't find this out until Monday evening when she appeared at the door asking if I still intended to take her to the pictures? I was fully occupied for the next three evenings and Mrs Watkiss became quite excited at the thought that she had matched us up. It was in fact the start of a beautiful friendship that lasted about six months.

The next weekend I finished work at 1.00 pm, dashed back to my lodgings, cleaned myself up and went to the station to catch the 2.30 pm train that took me straight through to Taunton for the weekend. I returned to work on the 6.12 am train from Taunton on Monday which got me back to Pontypool Road at about 8.20 am, leaving me just enough time to dash to my lodgings, put on my working overalls and get to work by 9.45 am.

Two weeks later I had a visit from Clarris who was home for the weekend from Clevedon. She told me that her boss and his family were going away the following weekend and would I care to break my journey there, with her, on Saturday night. I readily agreed and wrote to my mother and lied that I had to work early on Sunday morning saying that I wouldn't be home until late in the afternoon. On Saturday afternoon I caught the train to Bristol (Temple Meads) where I was met by Clarris. We did a bit of shopping, had tea in a cafe and then took the bus to Clifton Downs where we visited the Camera Obscura. The rotating lens in the roof of this little building projected a view of the surrounding countryside onto a large white saucer which was fixed to a stand in the centre of the room. Clarris was delighted by this, never having seen anything like it before. We caught the bus back to Temple Meads where we got into a Yatton-bound train, changing there for Clevedon. We arrived in this seaside town at about 8.00 pm and, after checking that everything was all right in the house, took a walk along a cliff path. We saw the lights of Newport reflected in the rippling water of the Bristol Channel and a sudden burst of light from a steel works where a massive crucible of molten metal was being poured. Clarris said that she was getting cold so we walked back to the house where we listened to the radio for a while. She then got up and made two mugs of cocoa and took them to the guest room where I was to sleep. She told me to make myself comfortable and went away to check that the house was securely locked for the night. I heard her come back to the bathroom but then she appeared in my room wearing her dressing gown. She sat on the side of the bed and we drank the cocoa. She took the tray and placed it on a table by the door and switched the light out. The next thing I knew she was sliding into bed with me between the sheets. I won't dwell on what happened next . . .

I slept very deeply that night and when I awoke it was daylight. Clarris was coming through the bedroom door holding a tray with eggs and toast on it. After breakfast I got up, washed and shaved and then helped Clarris to get the guest room tidy again. We went for another walk along the cliffs and shortly after returning to the house Clarris's sister called to see her. There was a lot of sisterly chatter over a cup of coffee during which I was eyed with some suspicion.

I said goodbye to Clarris and her sister and made my way to Clevedon station where I caught the 2.10 pm to Yatton which connected with a Bristol to Taunton service. I spent the rest of Sunday and most of Monday at home with my parents and then caught the 6.12 pm back to Pontypool Road. I had a week of nights to reflect upon the happenings of the previous weekend.

Clarris and I went on seeing each other until I was transferred back to Taunton. About a month later I received a letter from Clarris in which she enclosed a summons. Evidently she had cycled down Chapel Hill ignoring the 'Halt' sign at the bottom and was stopped by a policeman who demanded her name and address. She said that she had enclosed the summons so that I would know what one looked like in case I ever received one in the future! I didn't write back to her again but about two years later I heard that she had married. Not to a fireman, I might add.

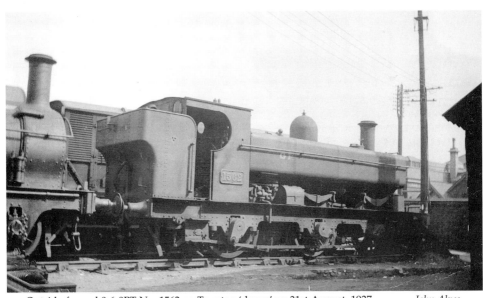

Outside-framed 0-6-0PT No. 1562 on Taunton 'dump' on 31st August, 1937.   *John Alves*

'1701' class 0-6-0PT No. 1760 performs shunting duties in West Yard, Taunton on 11th April, 1939.   *John Alves*

When I returned to Taunton I found myself working as a fireman in a Shunting Link. The oldest of the marshalling yards at Taunton was the down side yard at the east end of Taunton station and dealt with all the down freight trains calling at Taunton. These trains would arrive on the down goods loop which branched off from the main line at Taunton East Junction signal box. As soon as a down freight arrived at the home signal of Taunton East Loop signal box the 'train meeter' would detach any wagons for the yard. The train engine would pull these wagons forward over the connection to the down yard, where it would have to wait for shunting to cease. The shunting engine would then be sent up 'under the bell' which was a shunting bell mounted on the wall at the west end of the goods shed. The signalman in East Loop box working on the orders of the 'train meeter' would then set the road for the train engine to propel the wagons to be detached back into the yard under hand signals given by yard staff. Wagons containing traffic originating from Taunton, the branches or Bridgwater Docks that was to be sent on to other destinations in the West Country would be attached at this stage.

At this stage in my career the engines provided for shunting in the down yard were always one of the more powerful variety of Taunton's numerous pannier tanks which included Nos. 1760, 1899 or 2748.* This was before the arrival of any of the '57XX' class pannier tanks at Taunton, Nos. 9750 and 9751 being the first two that I can remember. On one Monday morning there was a bit of a mix up and No. 1909 ('850' class, built as a saddle tank at Wolverhampton 1881) arrived at the down yard for shunting at 5.00 am. When Mr Aplin, the yardmaster, arrived at 8.00 am he was on the phone straight away to Mr James at the shed to complain that No. 1909 wasn't powerful enough to deal with the work. So it was arranged that when No. 1760 arrived from the West Yard with a transfer the footplate crews were told to change over and No. 1909 went back there.

I remember that there were three regular drivers on the shunting engines in the down yard at this time; Joe Keating, Bill Seaford and Bill Pengelly. I believe all three had come off main line duties because of health reasons. The sidings in the down yard were numbered from the loop across to the cattle pens. Nos. 1 and 2 were reception roads, or possibly wagons waiting transfer to West Yard. Nos. 3 and 4 were for trains made up for the Barnstaple or Minehead branches, No. 5 was for vans waiting to be unloaded for Taunton trade deliveries, and No. 6 would contain coal for the Taunton coal merchants and also for the Taunton Corporation Electricity Department whose power station was situated in St James Street. No. 7 was the crane road where heavy items such as steel girders or timber would be offloaded by the mobile crane. No. 8 was a long siding which went right back into Messrs Pratt's, later the Esso Oil Company's depot. Oil for the Shell-Mex and BP companies was placed in a short siding at the west end of the large goods yard. From here there was an underground pipeline which connected with their depot in Canal Road. During this period Canal Road was still paved with rough granite sets which afforded the horses, used by the railway for haulage at this time, a better grip on the road; it wasn't asphalted over until the 1950s.

---

* 1760 – '1701' class, built as a saddle tank at Swindon 1892; 1899 – '1701' class, built as a saddle tanlk at Swindon in 1895; 2748 – '2721' class, built as a saddle tank at Swindon 1899.

'1901' class 0-6-0PT No. 1930 was put to use by Taunton Shed on 11th July, 1946 while *en route* from Swindon Works to its home shed St Blazey.   *John Alves*

Taunton East Yard signal box, with 2-6-0 No. 6368 on a class 'H' goods train detaches wagons and undergoes a crew change on 11th January, 1947. The train-meeter on the cab steps is Bill D'eath. This is the 9.05 am Rogerstone to Tavistock Jn loco. coal train.   *Roger Venning*

'County' class 4-6-0 No. 1018 *County of Leicester* is seen at Taunton with the 9.05 am Kingswear-Bradford on 5th July, 1946.   *John Alves*

A fine view of 'Castle' class 4-6-0 No. 5032 *Usk Castle* at Taunton on a Penzance-Manchester service, 28th September, 1946.   *R.C. Riley*

'Saint' class 4-6-0 No. 2903 *Lady of Lyons*, a Tyseley-allocated engine, is seen in the 'dead engine' sidings alongside Taunton Shed while awaiting repairs on 27th September, 1947.

Roger Venning

A siding ran westward off the No. 8 road into the cattle pens which could become very busy on Saturday afternoons. Taunton cattle market was located close by and animals that had been sold would be herded down Canal Road and up the ramp to the pens. The cattle traffic could be very heavy and it was not unusual for the yard to order an engine from the loco shed at short notice to run an extra to Banbury. These would depart at about 7.00 pm with each of the wagons bearing a label indicating when the cattle had last been fed and watered. Furthermore, if the cattle had not arrived at their destination within a specified time there were strict instructions that they were to be let out to be fed and watered and a record of this entered on the wagon label.

The goods shed handled the reception of all loose goods, crates of foodstuffs, sacks of corn and seed, and at certain times of the year a considerable amount of cattle cake. There were also bales of cloth for Van Heusen and the other shirt manufacturers in the town. Two tracks ran through the goods shed, one of which was spanned by four counterbalanced bridges which enabled merchandise to be brought across the shed to the platform face which formed the loading bay for the road vehicles. The shunter was responsible for seeing that the bridges were raised before an engine entered the goods shed. Incoming traffic would be shunted into the goods shed at about 6.00 am ready for the goods shed staff who came on duty at 7.00 am. Outgoing traffic from the shed would be cleared at about 7.00 pm for formation into trains which were being marshalled in the up yard. This yard was situated at the east end of the passenger station between the up goods loop and the No. 2 bay platform from where the Chard branch trains arrived and departed. The yard's main function was to marshal the local freight trains for Bridgwater, Yeovil, Chard and Charlton Mackrell on the Somerton cut-off. The up yard also serviced the needs of trains arriving on the up loop line.

A particular freight train that I can remember from this period was unofficially named the 'Flying Pig' and arrived on the up loop at about 6.00 each evening. It consisted of about 20 vacuum braked 'conflats' (container flat wagons) on which a white painted container was loaded. The containers were filled with meat bound for London's Smithfield Market. The train departed from Exeter and its last stop before Taunton was Lloyd Maunder's slaughter house beside the Tiverton branch at Tiverton Junction. This working was classified as an 'accelerated class E freight' and at this time was always hauled by a 'Castle' class locomotive returning to Old Oak Common as part of a balanced working.

Many trains ran through Taunton during the night and among them were the up and down Postal trains. The up train used to arrive in the station at 11.40 pm and one carriage was fitted with a built in letter box. Here any member of the public could post a letter and be sure that it would be delivered, first post, in London on the following morning. All letters posted this way had to have an additional ½d. stamp fixed to them in addition to the ordinary letter rate stamp of the day. The 8.05 pm Parcels train from Cardiff was nearly always hauled by one of the early breed of '29XX' 'Saint' class 4-6-0s, either No. 2902 *Lady of the Lake*, No. 2905 *Lady Macbeth* or No. 2908 *Lady of Quality*. Soon after this a fish train from Grimsby would roll in at about 2.00 am.

Fast fitted freight trains ran throughout the night. Both the 'Up' and 'Down Tip' consisted of 25 per cent vacuum braked stock and we would frequently see the 'Down Tip' thunder through the station as we took a meal break at about 3.00 am. There was also a succession of overnight passenger trains, the 9.35 pm Penzance to Paddington, the 9.50 pm Paddington to Penzance and the 12.20 am Paddington to Plymouth Newspaper train. During the late 1930s the Great Western Railway at Taunton was busy every hour of the day and night.

By November 1937 I had become the regular fireman to Frank Parsons and on this particular dark and dull afternoon we were working the late turn on the West Yard shunter. It must have been a Friday afternoon because the goods agent in the East Yard had spotted eight dirty cattle wagons and wanted them cleaned out right away in anticipation of the heavy traffic from Taunton Market on Saturday. Washing out was done by a gang of four men working from a special platform at the end of No. 6 siding in the West Yard. First we cleared all the stock out of this siding and then we went to the East Yard to collect the eight dirty cattle wagons ('Mex') which we shunted into No. 6 siding. While we and the under shunter had been away, the head shunter, Ern Davis, had taken the opportunity to trim and light his handlamp. Ern rode on the shunter's truck as we propelled the wagons into the siding for cleaning. He then uncoupled us and signalled us to draw away back over the points, which were set for No. 7 siding and locked to avoid any accidental shunt into No. 6 siding. He was walking towards the engine when there was a shout from one of the wagon washers, 'Stop that pig, Ern!'

Evidently there had been a pig that had been overlooked in the first wagon and as soon as the doors were opened it had made a bid for freedom, jumping down onto the ballast and shooting off up the track towards Ern. Without taking time for further thought our gallant head shunter acted instinctively, twisting the handle of his lamp he shone the red light at the pig and shouted "Whoa!' The pig's four legs went stiff and rigid and it stopped dead in its tracks.

The pig was caught and reloaded into a clean wagon which was sent back to the East Yard and was released into the cattle pens to be fed and watered while waiting be claimed. Those amongst us who believed in reincarnation thought that the pig must have been a driver in a former life, some of the longer-serving firemen thinking that they could actually name the individual concerned.

Early in my days as a fireman I found myself on a turn that took me to Watchet Harbour with a train to collect esparto grass that had been unloaded from a ship which had docked there. During a break in shunting to and from the quayside we were having our sandwiches and the subject of the longevity of Watchet's residents came up. Old Joe Knight, the shunter said, 'Oh ah, it was so bad the undertaker had gone bankrupt and they had to shoot somebody in order to start a cemetery!'

In these days where most households are heated by electricity, gas or oil, it is difficult to imagine the vast amounts of coal handled by the railway for local coal merchants. Coal was hauled from the colliery, often in its own wagons to various sidings in goods yards around the system. Here the coal merchant would unload the coal into sacks for distribution to his customers. The coal merchant was obliged to unload the coal from the wagons as quickly as possible, and if the wagons were not emptied promptly he would be charged 'demurrage' as a financial penalty for occupying railway wagons. This had come about because other traders had found it cheaper to keep their goods stored in railway vans rather than invest in expensive warehousing.

The humble coal wagon had been found to be a very uneconomic method of transporting coal as it only earned money for the railway company when it was loaded and travelling to its destination, it earned no money at all when empty and being returned to the colliery. In the 1930s each colliery had its own fleet of wagons and while very colourful and distinctive, they were a headache for the railway shunter. He had to segregate the various wagons according to their destinations. It was no good putting empty coal wagons from Blidworth, Cannock Chase or Monkton Colliery in a train load of empty wagons bound for South Wales. The wagons themselves were of a particularly ancient design, the body being made from timber and the axleboxes being lubricated with grease. They were not as free running as wagons running on oil lubricated boxes and therefore created problems by refusing to roll freely into sidings. During World War II all the private owner coal wagons were put into a common pool which meant any coal wagon could be sent to any colliery. By the end of the war the private owner wagons had reached the end of their lives and the onset of Nationalisation in 1948 saw their rapid withdrawal and replacement by the standard 16 ton steel mineral wagons which were owned by British Railways.

There were many other railway wagons that were only used for specialist traffic and hence returned empty to their owners. These included wagons used for bricks, china clay, salt and long open wagons named 'Tube' whose name informed you what they were used for. Naturally empty petrol tank wagons were returned empty to Avonmouth and empty milk tank wagons were returned each day to milk processing plants in the West Country and Wales.

One night our shift finished at 1.00 am. After cycling home I put my bicycle away, went in the porch, removed my dirty boots, got my key out, went indoors and through to the living room. The door of our living room would swing shut because the hinges were out of alignment but if the door was opened wide it would stay there. I opened the door wide, switched the light on and went through to the kitchen to make a cup of cocoa before going to bed. I had removed my dirty overalls in the kitchen and having made my drink I took it into the living room to sit down and have a biscuit by the glowing embers of the fire. Sitting on a dining room chair curled up and comfortable in front of the fire was our pet cat. On seeing me sit down the cat roused herself, sat up quietly putting her paws over the edge of the chair, silently slid to the floor. She walked across the room to the half open door where she raised one paw to the door and stood there while it swung shut. Then she turned around walked back to the chair in front the fire, climbed back up, curled herself around and glared at me before going back to sleep. I couldn't believe it; she seemed to be saying, 'Don't leave the door open!'

The former Great Western station at Highbridge looking south on 28th March, 1965. The Somerset & Dorset crossing is in the foreground.　　　　　　*J.C. Gillham*

Bristol Temple Meads station, with Bristol West (power box) in the foreground.　　*John Hodge*

Chapter Four

'Double-Home' Working

In the early 1900s the management of the railway realised that the only way to get maximum deployment of its footplate staff and guards was to arrange for them to work long distance trains from their starting point to their eventual destination. On arrival at the destination the footplate crews would sign off duty and after at least nine hours rest they would sign on again and work a train back to their home depot. This 'double home' working was a regular feature of the lives of many footplate crews and it survived as a working practice at Taunton up until the outbreak of World War II, when services became erratic and the system became unworkable.

The 'double-home' working which I worked as a member of the Junior Freight Link was one that took us as far as Bristol with a pick-up freight train. Signing on duty at 6.15 pm we would be off shed at 7.00 pm with a train which left the East Yard at 7.15. We would shunt at Durston, Bridgwater, Highbridge, Weston-super-Mare, Yatton and then run straight through to Bristol West Depot. Here we would leave the train and take the engine to Bristol, St Philip's Marsh Depot and sign off duty.

We then had to walk to a 'recognised lodging house' in Earlam Road, Bristol where would arrive at about 1.30 am. The front door key would be hidden under the door mat and after a quick wash we would go to bed which was sometimes still warm from the previous occupant. Hardly a hygienic arrangement by today's standards but one which the management thought adequate for footplate crews.

We would return to St Philip's Marsh Shed to sign on at 2.15 pm and prepare an engine to be off shed, light engine, at 3.00 pm to Bristol, West Depot. At 3.30 we would depart with a freight train for Weston-super-Mare, where on arrival we would draw into the goods yard, situated between the main passenger station and the excursion platforms at Locking Road. After we had completed the shunting and remarshalling of the train there was time for a meal break. Our departure time from Weston-super-Mare was dependent on a suitable interval being found for us to back our train out of the yard onto the down main and then make our way through the passenger station and on towards Highbridge. On arrival at the goods yard there we would detach a few wagons, some of which were bound for destinations on Somerset & Dorset Railway network. As soon as this operation was completed we were off to Bridgwater where the majority of the remaining wagons would be left. We were, however, still required to pick up a few late loadings here which we took on a mad dash to Taunton. On arrival at the East Yard at about 9.30 pm we would back the train into a siding and then take the engine to shed.

At this time the No. One Passenger Link had two 'double-home' workings to Paddington. One of these, already mentioned, was the 7.50 am to Paddington on Mondays, Wednesdays and Fridays, returning with the 9.15 am Paddington to Bristol express (which became the 12.45 pm stopping service thence to

'Castle' class 4-6-0 No. 5097 *Sarum Castle* with the 9.15 am Liverpool to Penzance express passing Fairwater bridge. This is the return working of the 8.45 am Plymouth-Manchester express, with a Salop engine and crew, on 26th September, 1947. Salop locomotives and crews worked 'down' on Mondays, Wednesdays and Fridays. Note the locomotive's tall safety valve bonnet.

Roger Venning

Taunton) on Tuesdays, Thursdays and Saturdays. On alternate days these trains would be worked by Old Oak Common crews. The other turn was the 6.35 am to Swansea on Mondays, Wednesdays and Fridays returning with the 7.15 am from Swansea on Tuesdays, Thursdays and Saturdays. On the alternate days the trains were worked by Landore crews.

In the Top Goods Link there were two 'double-home' turns, the first involved signing on duty at 10.00 am and relieving the Exeter men on the 8.30 am Exeter-Rogerstone train of empty loco-coal wagons. This would return the next day as the 5.15 am from Rogerstone to Laira with loaded loco-coal wagons. This loaded train was worked every day by Taunton men except on Mondays when it was worked by a Bristol crew for whom there was no balanced return working.

In those days pay day was on a Friday and I have seen a case of a fireman booking on at duty at 10.00 am for the 'double-home' turn to Rogerstone wanting his wages immediately so that he could give his waiting wife enough money to do the weekend shopping. He rightly claimed that by the time he returned on Saturday, signing off at 1.00 pm, the wages clerk would have gone home. He refused to leave the signing-on point until he was paid, but eventually had to be satisfied with a voucher to collect some cash from the station booking office to tide him over.

The other 'double-home' turn was the 11.05 pm express freight to Acton on Mondays, Wednesdays and Fridays, returning with the 10.15 pm ex-Acton on Tuesdays, Thursdays and Saturdays. One enterprising fireman who regularly worked this turn found that Lyons had a chocolate factory quite handy to Old Oak Common Shed, from where he was able to purchase a wide variety of confectionery at wholesale prices. He set up quite a business bringing back orders for his workmates, especially just before Christmas when the food compartment on the tender and sometimes even the top of the tender tank would be stacked up with cardboard boxes full of goodies!

I have been told that prior to World War I Taunton crews had a 'double-home' turn to Banbury and another to Lydney via the old Severn bridge. On this latter run they would travel via Stoke Gifford, Yate , Coaley Junction and the Sharpness branch. For the last part of the journey they would be working tender first , with no back sanding on the steep gradients that led up to the old Severn bridge.

To ensure that the practice survived for as long as it did the men who were rostered on these turns were looked after slightly better, in that at certain calling points a fireman from the local shed would be rostered to get up onto the tender and pull coal forward for them. At Taunton the fireman on the early turn West Yard shunter would sign on at 4.16 am to walk to the East Yard and pull coal forward on the tender of the 10.05 pm Acton express freight which was due to arrive at 4.31 am, usually hauled by one of the big '47XX' 2-8-0s. This was manned by Old Oak Common men on Tuesday, Thursday and Saturday and Exeter men on Wednesday and Friday.

Similarly the fireman of the 11.10 am to Yeovil was scheduled to pull coal forward on the 8.40 am Plymouth to Manchester, which was worked by Newton Abbot men on Monday, Wednesday and Friday and Shrewsbury men

'Castle' class 4-6-0 No. 5032 *Usk Castle* with the 8.45 am Plymouth to Manchester express at Taunton on 26th October, 1946. The Salop locomotive and crew worked the up train on Tuesdays, Thursdays and Saturdays. *Roger Venning*

'47XX' class 2-8-0 No. 4703 is seen with a very late running Acton to Plymouth goods train on 1st January, 1947, as it passes Obridge and is signalled for the goods loop lines. *Roger Venning*

on Tuesday, Thursday and Saturday. Other trains which ran throughout the day had to be covered by the loco foreman and he would instruct any fireman he had available to carry out this duty on such trains as the 7.00 am and 8.30 am ex-Plymouth and all the down trains from Paddington which were worked by 'double-home' men. At that time I didn't understand why we didn't perform this task for Wolverhampton men on the 10.40 am train from there to Penzance, the forerunner of the post war 'Cornishman', but I later found out that this task was done at Bristol.

On some occasions the foreman would find that he didn't have a spare fireman anywhere and then he would detail a couple of the cleaners to the station to pull forward coal on the necessary trains.

In general 'double-home' working was loathed and detested but this view depended on the home life and general outlook of the individuals involved. A lot of work was done after the end of World War II by ASLEF (the footplate staff union) to get rid of this working completely. Later when I was working at Dillington House a fireman from the North Eastern Region told me that his region depended heavily on 'double-home' working. He said that at his home shed they had introduced a train link of 20 turns, 19 of which were 'double-home' workings. The link was staffed on a voluntary basis, irrespective of seniority, and had been over-subscribed by 50 per cent!

As my route knowledge increased I came to realise that the Great Western signalling system gave the footplate crew, not only information as to whether the road ahead was clear, but also gave you advanced warning of which route you would be taking when you came to a junction. Here the highest of the signal arms would indicate the main line; any divergence from the main line, as in the case of going to a platform road, the signal arm would be placed slightly lower and to the left of the high main line signal arm. Sometimes the divergence could be to the right, as in the case of the quadrupled track at Reading East. Here the train would have to cross the up main line to run into the down relief platform road.

If you were approaching a junction where the diverging routes were judged be of equal importance and there was no speed restriction of less than 40 mph at the junction, there would be a distant signal for each route to give drivers advanced warning of the route set for the train and that all signals were clear for the block section ahead. These were called splitting distant signals. If the speed over one route at the junction was higher than the other, the distant signal arm for that route was placed at a higher elevation. If the speed over one route at the junction was less than 40 mph only one distant would be provided, worked only for the higher speed route. If both routes were less than 40 mph it would be fixed at caution. When working from Paddington to the West of England such signals could be found at Reading East giving advanced warning of the junction at Reading West. Further down the line at Heywood Road Junction, the right-hand signal would indicate to the driver that he going via Westbury station. The left-hand splitting distant signal would indicate that he was to travel via the Westbury Avoiding Line. Similarly at Clink Road Junction, the splitting distant signals would indicate if your route was via the Frome Avoiding Line (left-hand signal) or Frome station (right-hand signal).

A home signal was the signal that controlled the line approaching a signal box and protected a train standing ahead of it. A starting signal was a signal that controlled the line after the signal box had been passed and allowed a train to proceed into the next block section. In the case of signal boxes that controlled the movement of trains within stations there would be subsidiary signals which were located on the signal post beneath the main running signals. A subsidiary signal situated beneath a home signal would be a Calling On signal which would be lowered after the train had stopped to authorise the driver to pass the home signal at danger and inform him that the line towards the next stop signal was occupied and to proceed cautiously. These signals were much smaller and of a different pattern to the main running signals. When they were lowered they would reveal a small glass panel showing the letter 'C'.

If a subsidiary signal was placed beneath a starting signal controlling access to the section ahead it might reveal a letter 'S' when lowered. This would permit a driver to pass the starting signal at danger for shunting purposes only. It was also possible to find a subsidiary signal beneath a starting signal exhibiting a letter 'W' ('Warning') which would indicate to the driver that the section ahead could be entered but was only clear as far as the next home signal (i.e. there was not the usual 440 yds clear ahead of that signal). If there was no warning signal beneath a starting signal, the signalman would show a green flag in daylight or a green light in darkness before lowering the starting signal to indicate to the driver that he was being permitted to proceed 'under the warning' and that the section ahead was clear to the next home signal only.

Among other illuminated indications were 'R.A.' indicators which were situated ahead of a platform on a severe curve where it was impossible for the fireman to observe the 'Right Away' signal from the guard. One such signal was situated at the end of the down platform at Bath, as it was impossible for the fireman to see back along the platform.

Backing Signals were used to indicate to drivers or shunters that a 'wrong direction' movement was permitted, particularly in the case of shunting movements within a station area. These signals were about half the size of a main line signal and were painted red all over. They also had two holes, about 3 in. in diameter, punched out in the arms. These were superseded by elevated or ground disc signals and if two or more of these signals were placed one above the other the topmost signal would indicate clearance to the route to the extreme left, the second signal the line next to the left and so on. All point work operated by a signal box had a ground disc signal adjacent to them. A ground disc signal carrying a yellow arm and a yellow light could be passed in the stop position as in this position the line would run into a short dead end siding.

From all this you can see that a driver working on the GWR was kept exactly informed as to where he was going on the lowering of the appropriate signal. Great Western Railway drivers were at an additional advantage over their counterparts working for other railway companies because of the Automatic Train Control (ATC) apparatus fitted to their engines. The name was a misnomer as the control of the train was always in the hands of the driver, but it was a fundamentally good system which inspired confidence in all who used it. The equipment was fitted to all GWR engines except the smallest and most elderly shunting engines of the '19XX' and '20XX' classes and the '42XX' and '52XX' class of 2-8-0 tanks which spent most of their working lives on heavy coal trains, never venturing far from the Welsh Valleys. The locomotive equipment was fitted under the front buffer beam and consisted of a massive plunger switch designed to be pushed upwards when it passed over a metal ramp, which was situated in the middle of the track on the approach to a distant signal.

If the signal was clear the ramp was energised by a 16 volt circuit completed by a switch fitted to the rodding on the distant signal post and another switch fitted to the lever operating that signal in the signal box. The circuit held up an armature in the equipment box situated in the locomotive's cab which caused a bell to ring, indicating to the driver that the distant signal ahead was clear and as such all stop signals applying to the line on which he was running and worked from the same signal box as the distant were clear. This gave the driver the confidence to keep his train running at normal speed, enabling him to maintain booked timings even in thick fog.

If the signal was at the caution position the electric circuit would be broken and the ramp would be dead. The armature in the equipment box would be de-energised and a small steel lever, normally held up by the armature, would drop and in doing so would open a valve allowing air to be drawn into the vacuum brake system via a loud siren. The air entering the system would destroy the vacuum in the brake system and the brakes would be applied. The warning siren would be acknowledged by the driver who would lift a small lever on the side of the equipment box which would restore the steel bar across the armature, shutting off the air being drawn into the brake pipe through the siren.

When the driver acknowledged an ATC warning siren by lifting the lever he would reduce the speed of the train so that he was able to stop at the home signal. If this occurred in thick fog he would reduce the speed and use his route knowledge and familiar landmarks when approaching a signal that may be at danger. In fact both the driver and the fireman would have their eyeballs almost straining out of their sockets looking for the signal ready to whack over the vacuum brake handle over should the signal be at danger.

Having stopped at the signal it was the fireman's duty to walk to the signal box to advise the signalman of the train's position and to sign the train register to prove that Rule 55 had been carried out (this dealt with detention of trains on running lines). The signalman would place a metal collar over the handle of the signal lever to further remind him that the train was there. If a track circuit was provided at the signal, then there was no need for the fireman to go to the box.

The ATC equipment was very reliable but was susceptible to moisture in the form of fog, freezing rain or snow turning to ice which would adhere to the plunger causing it to jam in the raised position which resulted in the siren sounding continuously. In later years the contact shoe was modified to avoid this trouble. It was then fitted on a pivoted steel arm similar to an upside-down see-saw with strong springs retaining it in the down position. On 0-6-0 tank engines the modified shoe was fitted to a pressed steel plate attached to the underside of the leading axle boxes, this retained the shoe in the correct position above rail level.

0-6-0PT No. 9718 waits for signals at Obridge, on Taunton's goods loop lines with a stopping goods train to Chard in January 1947. The white shed on the right houses petrol 0-4-0 locomotive No. 24 in the Permanent Way Department yard.   *Roger Venning*

'45XX' class 2-6-2T No. 5542 leaves Norton Fitzwarren station with the 5.00 pm Taunton to Minehead train on 22nd October, 1947. The signal has already been returned to danger!
                                                                          Roger Venning

After Nationalisation in 1948 British Railways developed an electro-magnetic system known as AWS (Automatic Warning System) and this later became the standard equipment. As a dyed-in-the-wool Great Western man, even I had to admit that this system was superior as it gave a visual indication of the state of the last ground equipment over which we had passed and this served to remind the driver of the position of the distant signal he had just passed ('on' or 'off'). The new electro-magnetic AWS was fitted to the new main line fleet of diesel locomotives and during the 1960s and 1970s British Railways had to equip all its main lines to accommodate the new system including the former Great Western route. While steam traction by former Great Western or Western Region locomotives survived the old Great Western ATC had to be maintained.

With the outbreak of the World War II in September 1939 I was in my third year as a fireman and my rate of pay was 11 shillings a day. I had progressed as far as the Chard and Minehead Link which had many elderly or semi-convalescent drivers and I found myself firing to Dick Thomas who proved to be a genial character and generally a pleasure to work for. With the outbreak of the war we noticed that there were some rapid promotions for footplate staff but, being one of the youngest, I missed out and remained in the Chard and Minehead link. With the rapid build up in traffic some of the higher link firemen began to earn a significant amount of overtime which was evident when they began to wave the large white £5 notes they found in their weekly pay packets. Meanwhile yours truly was still earning the basic rate of pay for an 8 hour day. With so much extra traffic on the railway manpower became short and when footplate crews signed on for a booked duty there would be no guarantee that this would be the turn they would actually work. For some reason one day I found myself not firing with Dick Thomas but with another driver called Claude Philips with whom I worked the 9.30 am Chard Goods, a turn which got us back to shed about 4.00 pm. Having arrived back we found the foreman rushing around trying to make up an extra set of men to relieve a passenger train destined for Newton Abbot. When he saw Claude and me he hit upon an idea and asked us if we would like a couple of hours' overtime. Claude immediately said 'Yes' and he told us to relieve the No. 2 Link men when they returned from Yeovil to Minehead and back. They, in turn, would work the passenger train from Taunton to Newton Abbot. When we went to relieve these men on their return from Yeovil they were initially not at all happy about this arrangement until they made a quick mental calculation of the overtime they would earn. Our trip to Minehead also ensured that we made 12 hours that day.

Not long after this I found myself paired with Driver Tom Gill a widower who didn't want to work any overtime at all. He would go out of his way to make sure we finished in no more than the basic eight hours whenever possible.

Signing on for Control Relief at 4.00 am we were ordered to relieve a down freight train in the goods loop at about 7.00 am. This train was headed by 'Castle' class 4-6-0 No. 5077 *Eastnor Castle* (renamed *Fairey Battle* in October 1940) and, typical of this period, we struggled from loop to loop until we eventually arrived at Tiverton Junction. Having spent over an hour waiting in the platform road the signalman informed us that Control had decided that we were to put the train in the down refuge siding because there was no hope of dealing with it immediately. Our orders were then for us to proceed light engine to Exeter. We set back into the down refuge siding and the guard secured the train and cut off the engine. I put one headlamp on the tender lamp bracket and one on the front of the engine and we pulled down into the platform road again and stopped. Here Tom called out to the signalman, 'Taunton engine and Taunton men, back light to Taunton!' Immediately the guard was displeased because he was an Exeter man, but Tom reassured him that there would be a passenger train along soon and he could get home on that. So the signalman set the points for us and we returned home to Taunton where we disposed of the engine on the fire pit. As we were taking the lamps and the keys we were met by Mr James, the head foreman, who was pleased to see this engine back on shed which he immediately stopped for boilerwashing and an M.P. 11 examination. We signed off on the dot at 12.00 midday and I only earned eight hours pay again!

One of the early wartime economy measures that affected us on the footplate was the alterations made to the engine's blower jets. The blower exhausted its steam via angular ring of holes in the base of the chimney. The jets were angled upwards and the steam escaping from them when the blower valve was opened created a partial vacuum in the smokebox and thus created a draught through the firebed. This in turn made the fire burn brighter and hence burn more fuel. The management decided that it would reduce the number of jets in order to reduce the amount of fuel wasted by the indiscriminate use of the blower. The effect their actions had was for a horrible wailing or screaming noise to emanate from the chimney when the blower was turned on. The noise was embarrassing and irritating and the footplate crews wouldn't use the blower unless it was absolutely essential and so it probably had the desired effect.

I didn't realise what an idyllic world I had been living in as the next five years would bring long hours of duty, food shortages and many hours of boredom waiting in sidings. I have already mentioned the massive increase in the amount of traffic being carried by the railway and the large number of extra trains required to carry it. These comprised not only the regular goods train but also train loads of military equipment. Local traders, uncertain for the future supply of basic materials, filled their warehouses with additional stocks creating a shortage of freight rolling stock. The freight yardmasters became so concerned about the return of empty wagons that they would phone the Loco. Department and order a special train at a moment's notice. On one such occasion when I was firing to George Smith on the 3.00 pm spare shift the foreman came to us and instructed us to prepare '2251' class 0-6-0 No. 2268 to haul a special from Taunton East Yard to Bristol, West Depot. He added that we were to be sure that we brought the engine back with us as it was needed for the Barnstaple service on the following morning. We quickly went about our tasks and were soon off shed and up the loop to the East Yard. Here we set back into the No. 2 road on the up side. The shunter coupled us to the waiting train and the guard came up and gave us the load as being 55 empty wagons. This particular train of wagons had been blocking the yard preventing the shunters from dealing with the regular traffic. Once we were ready the guard went to the East Loop signal box and told the signalman we were going. I put up 'H' headcode headlamps, one on the chimney bracket and the other on the bracket above the middle of the buffer beam, indicating we were a train carrying a through load to a destination. In no time at all the signals were lowered, George eased open the regulator and we were pulling out of the yard and onto the up loop.

We slowly approached Taunton East Junction signal box as there is a falling gradient here, but we needn't have worried because the signals were clear for us to proceed onto the up main line. The time was around 6.10 pm, and soon we were being overtaken by the up 'North Mail' on the up relief line. We realised that the signalman had taken a calculated risk in letting us out on the main line at this time because an express service for Paddington was due along this track at 6.25 pm, and so George accelerated our train away as quickly as he could. The Creech Junction distant signal was clear which meant that we would be crossing over from up main to up relief at Cogload where the up relief became the main line to Bristol. The section from Cogload to Durston is quite short and the up 'North Mail' would have cleared it by the time we got to Cogload, so with no need to hang about we rattled over the junction pointwork at Creech St Michael. There was no need to take water from Cogload troughs and with the signals clear we did not slacken our pace through the crossover there which was laid out for fast running.

The 'North Mail' would now be well past Meads Crossing by the time we were approaching Durston and with No. 2268 steaming well with a 'haycock' fire and the pressure just below the red line at 195 lb. per sq. in. we ran confidently on to Bridgwater. Here we ran through straight through the station and on towards the new British Cellophane factory. As we approached the bridge that carried the S&D's Bridgwater branch over our main line we saw their 0-6-0 engine and two coaches. Onwards we sped to Dunball and past the new signal box at Huntspill, built to serve the sidings of the Royal Ordnance depot at Puriton. With my head down feeding the hungry fire the next lurch I felt was when we crossed the S&D's tracks at Highbridge. Looking forward now from my side of the footplate along this straight and level track I could see a succession of clear signals through Brent Knoll and on to Brean Road Halt. At Bleadon & Uphill we were pleased to see the that the up distant for Uphill Junction was clear which meant we were routed via the avoiding line. Having passed through the deep cutting and over the junction we noticed the new signal box and sidings being laid in for the aircraft factory. There were no trains due in or out of Weston-super-Mare at this time and this meant that we had a clear road over Worle Junction and on to Puxton & Worle where I noticed a train of shining stainless steel tankers standing in the sidings of the milk factory.

All the time I had been feeding the fire with half full shovels of coal as these engines steam well when the fire is fed a little and often. Between Huish Crossing and Yatton the line is still level and as we speed through the platforms we saw the auto-train for Clevedon in the up bay platform, and at the down bay platform a train for Cheddar, Wells and Witham waiting for a connecting service from Bristol. As we passed the sidings between Yatton East and Claverham the gradient climbs gently to a summit at Flax Bourton. Later during the war we would spend many hours waiting here for a path into the reception sidings in Bristol. However, tonight the sidings were empty and our engine continued to steam well with the

'Dean Goods' class 0-6-0 No. 2527 passes under Cogload flyover with a local goods train on 31st August, 1939.
John Alves

Worcester engine 'ROD' class 2-8-0 No. 3027 works a down class 'E' goods train to Plymouth passing Taunton Shed's coaling stage at Whitehall on the goods loop, 30th November, 1946.
Roger Venning

left-hand injector feeding continuously all the way from Cogload, keeping the water well up in the gauge. As the gradient began to arrest our progress I cut the injector to give George full boiler pressure for the road ahead to Nailsea and Flax Bourton. I deliberately kept the injectors off all the way through the short tunnel and past the intermediate block signal and we began to drop down the falling gradient in the long cutting beyond. George still needs full boiler pressure to control the train with the steam brake because South Liberty signal box will have its distant on as almost all freight trains run on the loop from here to Bristol, West Depot. Once the train was on the loop I put the injectors on again to prevent the boiler from blowing off excess steam at the safety valves. We pulled up through the reception road and our train was met by a shunter who cut off our engine and told us to proceed to shed. George told him that the engine had to go straight back to Taunton and so arrangements were made for us to proceed along the Portishead branch as far as West Loop Junction, where we reversed back towards Parson Street Junction signal box on the line that formed a triangle. We were now facing the right way for our return to Taunton, where we arrived after an uneventful light engine run at about 9.00 pm. I locked the tools away and took the headlamps and keys to the stores while George reported back to the same shift foreman who had given us the job earlier that afternoon. The foreman, whose shift did not end until 11.00 pm, thought we had come as passengers from Bristol and started to curse and swear at George for not bringing the engine back with him. As soon as George was able to get a word in edgeways and explain that the engine was safe on the coal road his mood changed to one of delight and he let us both go home early.

Even though this period has been characterised as the 'Phoney War' the traffic quickly grew to the extent where the full capacity of the line was being used and Control was forced to use some unorthodox routes to ensure that the trains got through. Many Bristol bound freights were routed via Westbury such was the density of traffic on the direct line.

Signing on one morning at 7.00 am while working under the Control Relief arrangements, we were not given a job until 8.15 am when we were sent to the up goods loop to relieve a train of sugar beet bound for the processing plant at Wallerscote, which we would work as far as Westbury. Here we found an old ROD 2-8-0 No. 3026 and we relieved its Exeter-based crew. We took water and soon got the road to proceed as far as the East Loop signal box where the signalman asked us if we knew the route to Athelney via Durston and Lyng Halt. Having regularly worked over the Yeovil branch this was no problem and so we trundled off to Taunton East Junction box where we had to wait while the 8.48 am auto-train for Castle Cary departed from the station via the up relief line. As soon as this train had cleared the section the signals were lowered for us to follow on the same track, leaving the up main line clear for the 7.00 am Plymouth to Paddington which departed from Taunton station at 9.15 am. The RODs were always rather sluggish machines but soon we were ambling along at about 30 mph. It seemed unusual to be running through Creech St Michael on the up relief line when we knew we were bound for Westbury but there were no facing points to cross from the up relief to the up main at Cogload Junction. A short time after we had passed Cogload box we saw the exhaust steam from the 7.00 am Plymouth to Paddington going up the main line, and then we found

Castle Cary station looking towards London. The line approaching from the left is from Taunton, while that from the right is from Yeovil. This view shows the later signal box which had replaced an earlier one which had been destroyed during World War II.

British Rail

Athelney signal box.   *Exe Rail*

that we had to stop at Durston because the 8.48 am departure from Taunton to Castle Cary was waiting to get onto the main line at Athelney and follow the up express. It was not long before the signalman brought us the staff for the single line section along the branch to Athelney and then to Westbury with our heavy load. The rest of the journey was uneventful but the start had been quite remarkable, due to the quick thinking of the signalman who recognised the importance of keeping the traffic moving.

As 1940 passed into 1941 the whole system seemed to be so overloaded that it was slowly grinding to a complete halt. We would spend many hours waiting in sidings and to relieve the boredom I would clean the fire by breaking up the lumps of clinker that formed on the firegrate, hooking out the larger pieces with the pricker and shovel them out onto the ballast. I would shovel all the old stale coal on the back of the tender to the front. This would at least ensure that we got some fresh coal when we next went to shed. A typical case was one evening when we were in a queue of trains in the long loop between Yatton East and Claverham, all of which were waiting for a path into the marshalling yards in Bristol. Recognising that we could expect a long delay the guard came up to see my driver, Tom Gill, and together they went off to the signal box for a gossip with the signalman, leaving me to look after the engine. I went through the familiar routine I mentioned, breaking up clinker and shovelling coal forward and then set the blackout sheets. Now I intended to make myself comfortable but before doing this I had to black down the fire which I did by shovelling a great pile of this stale coal into the firebox , forming a large mound on the centre of the grate. While I was doing this I had the injector on filling up the boiler so that everything would be right for me to have a nap. I flipped down the fireman's seat and propped my shovel upside down against it. From our allowance of cotton waste I formed a cushion which I placed against the heel of the shovel. I now sat on this cushion with my right elbow on the seat and my head resting on my hand. I promptly fell sound asleep. In the meantime it had got dark and about an hour later I suddenly awoke in a state of complete disorientation. In my semi-dazed state I mistook the huge pile of coal in the tender for the large pile of stale coal I had previously shovelled into the firebox. I looked at the coal and thought the fire had gone out. I was so convinced of this that I actually got up and was feeling the coal on the tender with my hand to see if it was still warm. It was only then that it dawned on me that I was able to see the coal because of the light of the fire from the firebox behind me. The sense of relief at finding that this was a ridiculous mistake made me laugh aloud at myself.

One enterprising fireman had been waiting in the Claverham loop for many hours when daylight began to break. In the gloom he notice a small farm nearby with about four cows grazing on the dewy grass. Taking his tea can he climbed down from the footplate and over the fence and into the field where he succeeded in milking one of the cows. Returning with his tea can filled with fresh milk he poured some of it into his own milk bottle and some into the one belonging to his driver. The remainder in his tea can he rested on the fire where it soon boiled. Into this he placed some stale crusts of bread and shared this makeshift meal with his driver and so managed to stave off the pangs of hunger for a few more hours.

Working conditions gradually deteriorated; with long hours, food rationing and the uncertainty of setting off for work with no idea of when you might return, it is not surprising that our morale soon hit rock bottom. I can remember signing on duty at 12.00 midday and not signing off again until 2.30 pm the next day. We were not as fortunate as factory workers who enjoyed works canteen facilities and even the forces had refreshment stands at various stations but their staff refused to acknowledge the part we were playing in the war-effort. One well known organisation had a refreshment bar on Bristol (Temple Meads) station which refused to sell me a cup of tea after I had been on duty for over 14 hours. A sailor standing nearby took pity on me and bought one for me which was served up in a glass jam jar. Needless to say I was very grateful!

The wartime Ministry of Food made no recognition of the hard physical work endured by footplate crews and we had to make do with the same ration as other civilians. Needless to say we never missed an opportunity to supplement these rations by whatever means, legal or illegal, when it presented itself. The best source of additional rations was out on the rural branch lines where the station staff always knew of someone with rabbits for sale or a farmer with surplus eggs. It was very satisfying to come home with a brace of rabbits or a cabbage 'nicked' from a field beside the railway.

We were stopped in the loop near Morebath Junction on the Barnstaple branch when I saw a rabbit struggling in a wire trap close to the railway fence. I got down from the footplate, collected the rabbit and put him out of his misery. On returning to the footplate I gutted it with my pocket knife and emptied the entrails onto the coal. My driver kicked up hell about the smell and the mess but I soon shovelled this into the firebox and hosed down the footplate with the 'pet pipe'.

Chapter Five

Wartime Experiences

From about 1940 onwards the war really began to make itself felt. Materials became very scarce and we found that even basic bits of footplate equipment began to suffer because of this. Perhaps the worst affected was the simple gauge glass lamp. The original lamps had a clear front glass and side glasses were coloured, red on the left and green on the right-hand side. The coloured glass became unobtainable and a new pattern of gauge lamp emerged from Swindon Works with plain tin sides. Then when tinplate fell in short supply damaged lamps returned to Swindon for repair took months, if ever, to return to our shed. Fortunately for us there was a storekeeper at Bristol, Bath Road Shed (BRD), whose name was Donald who took on the job of repairing these essential pieces of equipment. He was a dab hand with tin snips and a soldering iron and was able to scrounge pieces of glass from a variety of sources. He was particularly delighted when somebody gave him a box of about 50 old glass plate negatives and when he was not issuing oil and stores he would sit down at a table and shape the glass to the prescribed size for the gauge lamps, nibbling away at the thin glass with a pair of specially sharpened pincers which were always kept highly polished. One could always tell if your lamp had been repaired by Donald because it had a photographic negative for the side pieces. He was a particularly obliging person, even being prepared to cut you a circular piece of glass for your bicycle lamp or pocket torch.

My first wife and I married at Easter 1940 but because of the national emergency I was only permitted to have one day off duty at the time. We had to wait until June to take our honeymoon when I had a week's leave and we spent the time at Sandgate near Folkestone where we stayed with my mother-in-law. To my delight I found that Hythe, the eastern terminus of the Romney, Hythe and Dymchurch Railway was just a mile or so down the road and I managed to persuade my wife to take a journey with me on this world famous miniature railway. We were able to travel to New Romney and arrived back at Hythe at about 4.00 pm to be greeted by the wail of the air raid sirens. We started to walk up the road but an air raid warden on a bicycle hailed us and told us to take cover in the station building. We heard the sound of aircraft overhead followed by bursts of machine-gun fire but could not tell if anything had been hit. This was to be our first taste of the war!

During that week we walked into Folkestone and went down to the harbour where we watched an incredible variety of boats coming in from across the channel. They were heavily laden with troops who had been evacuated from Dunkirk as the German army had advanced towards the French coast. We could see that the soldiers were not only British but also French, Dutch and Polish who had been fighting the Nazis. The ships that brought them back to England varied from fancy yachts to old coal boats and the relief on their faces at being brought back was clearly visible. Across the channel the battle continued to rage. We could hear the explosions from the opposing artillery and

2-6-2T No. 4136 banks a down goods train up Wellington bank. Train engine 2-8-0 No. 3845 is about to enter Whiteball tunnel on 22nd April, 1951.

Pursey Short

as darkness fell the flashes illuminated the horizon. At first the German army was still grouped some distance south-west of Dunkirk but each night it was possible to judge the speed of their advance from the flashes of their artillery positions. The scene on the station was hectic with train after train of diverse stock headed by every locomotive the Southern Railway could roster evacuating the troops to inland bases. When it was our time to leave we were fortunate to be able to board a Victoria-bound train which left at about 6.00 on the Saturday evening. Because all the troop trains had priority we did not arrive in the capital until about 1.00 am on Sunday. Somehow we made our way across London and arrived at Paddington station to be told that the first train to Taunton was not until 10.30 am. We spent the next nine hours just kicking our heels at the station but as dawn broke we were amazed to see a host of barrage balloons floating over the city. These were to be the first of many that we would see over various cities during the next four years. Eventually we got away from Paddington and where glad to arrive home in Taunton at about 3.00 pm on 16th June, 1940.

We settled down to the routines of married life and my wife got used to the rigours of being married to a railway fireman. I had to leave for work at all hours of the day and night and she supported me by preparing my grub box with whatever food was available to us under the austere food rationing regime imposed on us all. While some additional dairy produce found its way home from local farms and a productive garden ensured a good supply of vegetables, my wife had to learn rapidly the art of skinning rabbits! I was still allowed one week's holiday a year but journeys to the seaside were out of the question because travel to within three miles of the coast was prohibited. Our first family holiday did not occur until 1953.

Whether it was wartime or peacetime heavy freight trains had always needed a banking engine to get them over the top of Whiteball Bank. It wasn't that the train engines were not powerful enough to take the average freight train over the top unassisted, but the time it would have taken to do so would have created a huge backlog of traffic. Taunton was the junction where West Country-bound trains from Paddington and the Midlands met and, from Norton Fitzwarren onwards, there was only a double track of railway. The regular engines allocated to these banking turns were the '51XX' class 2-6-2 tanks and at that time were either Nos. 4113, 4117, 4136 or 5172. If these engines were not available we might have a '63XX' 2-6-0 tender engine and I can even remember banking with 'Grange' class 4-6-0 No. 6868 *Penrhos Grange* on one occasion. The night turns were always the busiest and two engines were always on hand, one being off shed at Taunton at 9.45 pm and the other at 10.30 pm. I worked so frequently on these turns that I think I can claim to have known every rail joint between Wellington and Whiteball on a personal basis.

The winter of 1942 found me firing to Tom Gill in the Wellington Banker Link. Unusually we had been given a '63XX' 2-6-0 tender engine for the 10.30 pm night banking shift which was not as warm as the enclosed cab of the '51XX' 2-6-2 tanks, so for once we were glad of the blackout sheets. There was a freight train already waiting for us when we arrived at Wellington, so we buffered up to the rear of the brakevan, gave the customary two 'crows' on the whistle and

Mogul No. 6317 banks a down goods train hauled by Severn Tunnel Junction-based 2-8-0 No. 3850 up Wellington bank on 25th March, 1951. *Pursey Short*

Didcot-allocated Stanier class '8F' No. 8406 is at a stand in Victory Siding with a down 'H' class goods to Plymouth (Tavistock Jn), while waiting for the main line to clear, 6th July, 1946. *Roger Venning*

were soon on our way up the bank. On arriving at Whiteball we were rapidly crossed over and dispatched back to Wellington. Running back towards the tunnel I opened the firehole doors wide to warm up the cab and as I turned around I saw from the light of the fire a pair of shiny black boots standing on the shovel plate of the tender. Having been warned about the possibility of sabotage to the railways by 'Fifth Columnists' and their like, I armed myself with a large spanner and raised the back sheet of the blackout screen. There stood a bewildered young man in Naval uniform who rapidly explained that he had to get back to Plymouth. When we had stopped at Wellington he had climbed up into the back of our tender with the intention of staying there until we arrived at Plymouth. To his dismay he found that we had only come as far as Whiteball and now he was heading back to Wellington again. There were a lot of westbound trains that night and the signalman had kept us on the up main line ready to cross over as soon as the next train arrived. A pair of headlights shone out in the darkness and the 9.55 am Bristol West Depot to Tavistock Junction rolled into the station. We crossed over and came up behind the brakevan and I had to get down from the footplate to put the red glass from the front of the engine back into the tender lamp again. I told the lad to come with me and fortunately for him I was able to negotiate a ride back to Plymouth with the guard in the brakevan.

Before the outbreak of World War II you had to go to Bristol or Exeter if you wanted to see locomotives belonging to the other railway companies. We never dreamed we would see anything other than Great Western engines at Taunton, but then in 1943 LMS '8F' 2-8-0s made their appearance and I soon had my own first hand experience with one of these. My driver and I were on yet another Control Relief turn signing on at 3.00 am. We then walked to the East Yard where we reported to the relief controller in the inspector's office. Our cabin in this yard was then a spare brake van parked up against the stop blocks in the cattle siding. After sitting around for about an hour we were told to relieve a freight train standing in the down goods loop line and I was amazed when I found that the engine was an LMS '8F' 2-8-0. We climbed up onto the footplate and were greeted by the Bristol crew we were relieving. This was the first non-Great Western footplate that I had ever been on and I had to ask the Bristol fireman for a quick conducted tour. How different everything was! For a start the driver drove from the left-hand side and so the fireman's tools were on the right-hand side. Not only was the water scoop handle on the front of the tender behind the driver and the tender handbrake on the right but they were mounted vertically with the operating shafts being driven through a pair of bevel gears. The injector water valves were just bits of bent steel mounted on the front of the tender which you pulled up to operate and pushed down to shut off. In later years when these engines got rough the fireman would have to keep a close eye on the injector overflow pipe because the vibration would shake these valves shut. It became quite common to see them tied up in the open position with an odd piece of string.

I also found that the firehole was fitted with a firing flap which was very similar to our own engines but not as large. It only closed off the bottom half of the firehole and furthermore it was not fitted with a chain for opening and closing between each shovelful. I could only assume that it was meant to remain turned up, meaning that you would have to fire the coal over the top. The problem was that we were still being issued with the large GW shovel which was far too big for this technique and so the flap was left turned down and the firehole doors were used.

Turning to the boiler backhead, all the control handles operated by the driver were on the left and this created the immediate disadvantage for me of having to fire left-handed. I am a naturally right-handed person and was accustomed to holding the shovel with my left hand on the shaft and as much as I tried to fire the other way around I just couldn't get it right. Having struggled with this during many later trips I ended up adopting the technique used by the LMS firemen, sometimes referred to as the 'Derby Charge', which involved opening the firehole doors and shovelling in as much as possible in one go and then hoping for the best.

The injector steam valves were situated in a conventional position on a manifold at the top of the boiler but were different in that their operating handles were brass wheels with a single straight spigot on the rim. In the centre of the manifold was a valve with just a 2 inch square stem and no handle. Obviously this was the manifold shut-off valve and the Bristol fireman warned me not to touch this as it would cut off steam to everything including the brakes. The last thing I got him to explain was a large piece of equipment fitted to the boiler backhead above the firehole and beneath the regulator. This he told me was the sand gun which would spray sand onto the tubeplate and up the tubes to scour them clear of soot and ashes, he emphasised that it was only to be used when the engine was working really hard. I was inquisitive to find out more about this accessory and as soon as he was gone I examined it more closely. There was a hand wheel which could be turned in either direction to aim the nozzle of the gun at any part of the tubeplate. A pipe led away to a sand container on the fireman's side of the backhead where the contents were kept dry by the heat of the boiler. Another pipe led away to a valve which fed live steam to the nozzle to blast the sand into the firebox. I hoped that I might get an opportunity to play with this gadget sometime during our trip to Newton Abbot.

Before we could set off for Newton Abbot we had some wagons to detach and I saw my driver apply the steam brake. The valve for this was on the right-hand side of the vacuum brake ejector and was operated by a handle about 1 ft long, by which it was possible to actuate the steam brake quite independently of the vacuum brake. The Bristol men had filled the tender water tank before we had relieved them and so, as soon as the shunter had cut off the wagons to be detached, he waved us ahead with his handlamp. As the signals were all on my driver's side I spent some time trying to build up a good fire from my normal position on the left-hand side of the footplate. Once the shunting operations were over we set back onto the train and the guard came up and gave us the load. The signals were cleared, my driver wound the reversing screw into full forward gear and gingerly opened the regulator, as he was still far from familiar with this sort of engine. As soon as we were moving I took the gauge glass lamp and exchanged signals with the guard and then returned to the right-hand side of the footplate and tried to get used to these different surroundings. The engine appeared to be relatively new and was still in good condition. It moved away strongly with hardly any of the knocks and bangs that were so evident in many of our engines which at this time were suffering from inadequate maintenance.

I was pleased to observe that the gap between cab and tender was closed by a spring-loaded steel door. This was a luxury we weren't used to, having to contend with fierce draughts blowing around you most of the time. As we ran slowly around the back of Taunton Shed on the goods loop I thought it was time to add some more coal to the fire. Opening the firehole doors I noticed that the bit I had added earlier was now burning through quite nicely, so I apologised to my driver for having to fire over his side and then did another round of firing. Soon after the safety valves roared open and so I lifted the tender water valve handle and turned on the steam valve for the right-hand injector. I looked over the side to watch the overflow and was impressed by how quickly the injector picked up without wasting a drop of water. This was the exhaust steam injector which was unusual in having only one steam valve whereas the Great Western variety had two, the centre one which was the main valve and the left-hand one of the three being the supplementary valve for when the regulator was shut. This '8Fs' exhaust injector changed over automatically when the regulator was shut. I later discovered that these injectors where manufactured by Gresham and Craven whereas our GWR engines were equipped with Davies and Metcalfe injectors. Years later I found that 'Castle' class 4-6-0 No. 4091 *Dudley Castle* was fitted with a Gresham and Craven exhaust injector and that this was fitted with only two steam valves on the manifold.

One drawback with this '8F' was that it wasn't yet fitted with the Great Western ATC and so we had to look out for every distant signal because there was no audible warning for us. The traffic department must have had a purge which resulted in us having a clear run to Wellington where we stopped for the banker to come onto the rear of our train. The banking engine gave two 'crows' on its whistle and my driver reached up for the whistle chain but couldn't find it. Eventually he caught hold of a lever which he could only assume was the whistle valve and then we heard a low husky note that sounded like a ship's fog horn. He opened the regulator again and, as soon as we were underway, wound the reverser back to about 35 per cent cut-off. He was obviously satisfied that I was on top of the firing because he then opened the regulator wide and we began to get stuck into the climb to Whiteball. We had not yet felt the effect of the banker, or it could simply have been that they weren't doing their fair share, but here was the opportunity for me to see what the sand gun could do. I turned on the steam valve and opened the lid of the sand container where I could see that its contents were disappearing quite rapidly. I got hold of the operating wheel and turned it two full turns spraying sand all over the tubeplate. Daylight was just breaking and my driver had had his head out of the cab side window, but now he hastily pulled it inside and demanded to know what the hell I was doing. I told him I had set the sand gun going to clean the tubeplate and the tubes. He then told me to look what was happening as soot and ashes were raining down on the engine and when I looked back along the train the dawn had been completely blacked out over Rockwell Green by a pall of thick smoke. I quickly shut off the steam valve and when I lifted the lid of the sand container

The station approach at Wellington on the down side, shortly after the rebuilding of the station in 1932. *British Rail*

Whiteball Siding signal box. *Exe Rail*

it was almost empty. Obviously it had cleared a good deal of old rubbish off the tubeplate, tubes and flues. The engine steamed well, I was getting the hang of the firing and the use of the exhaust injector and I am glad we all came through this test with flying colours. We went through the tunnel and over the top of the bank, maintaining full pressure against the injector, and then enjoyed a clear run until we were pulled into the platform loop at Cullompton to wait a for path into Exeter. The rest of our first encounter with an '8F' was uneventful and soon after arriving at Hackney Yard the engine was cut off from the train and we proceeded to shed at Newton Abbot.

LMS '8F' 2-8-0 No. 8433 was eventually allocated to Taunton, where it soon suffered serious damage to its left-hand front cylinder when a fireman attempted to get the engine moving on the shed exit road. Unknown to him the cylinder cock that should have drained this end of the cylinder had seized shut and when the engine slipped, the trapped condensation smashed the front cylinder cover. If this sort of damage had occurred to a GW engine it would have been repaired within 24 hours but in this case the engine was stood idle on shed awaiting the arrival of a replacement cylinder cover for over two weeks.

A wide variety of engines began to be seen on through freight workings and even Exeter Shed was loaned an engine from the Southern to assist with 'the war effort'. This turned out to be a member of the 'Remembrance' or 'N15X' class of 4-6-0. They had originally been built as 4-6-4 tank engines by the London, Brighton & South Coast Railway between 1910 and 1922 to a design of L.B. Billinton. By the early 1930s the Southern Railway had electrified many of the lines over which they operated and these large tank engines became surplus to requirements. They were subsequently rebuilt as 4-6-0 tender engines between 1934 and 1936 and sent to the former LSWR section of the Southern Railway where, after initial trials with fast passenger trains, they were soon relegated to less demanding work on milk trains and other fitted freight workings.

Exeter was allocated No. 2329 *Stephenson* where the loco crews explained that its lack of power was due to a combination of large diameter driving wheels, small grate area and low working pressure. It was said that they were called the 'Remembrance' class because they were unforgettably useless!

The first time that I had any contact with this engine was when I was firing on the Wellington Banker. At about 7.00 one evening the main line signals were lowered and within five minutes a freight train was heard approaching. As No. 2329 *Stephenson* hove into view it appeared to be going quite well but with only 20 wagons that was to be expected. It ran through Wellington station and we settled down to another cup of tea but after a period of about 15 minutes the signals were lowered for us to pull out of the refuge siding. We proceeded as far as the signal box where the signalman stopped us with his red flag. He told us that the freight train had stopped at Beam Bridge finding itself unable to make the grade. He instructed us to pass the signals at danger, proceed into the section to find the train and then bank it up to Whiteball. We soon found the guard who had walked back about half a mile to protect his train in the rear. We picked him up and carried on to buffer up against the brake van. In no time at all we had the train under way and experienced no further difficulty up the bank.

'N15X' 'Remembrance' class 4-6-0 No. 2333 *Remembrance* at Nine Elms Shed on 13th August, 1947.   *Roger Venning*

LNER 'O1' class 2-8-0 No. 3874 at Colwick on 12th July, 1947.
                                                John P. Wilson/Rail Archive Stephenson

This sort of incident contributed to this engine's lousy reputation and like most other crews we would stop for assistance wherever it was provided when given No. 2329 for any working. When using this engine on the Exeter to Swindon freight via the Berks & Hants line we would even insist on a banker from Castle Cary to Brewham. If you were working a Paddington-bound train on a Sunday morning and were relieved at Westbury you would be stranded for several hours. The earliest service back to Taunton left at midday which was a local train to Frome. Here you could catch the branch service via Radstock, Midsomer Norton and Hallatrow to Bristol from where you got home, eventually.

After signing on at 3.00 on a Sunday morning to work a train to Westbury we found that we were one of three crews and three guards all looking for a return working back to Taunton. As we were the last crew on duty we were instructed to go to Westbury Shed, get an engine and then go to the yard where they had found a brake van which would form a special train back to Taunton. When we reported to the Westbury Shed foreman he told us to take No. 2329, appearing to be pleased at the prospect of getting rid of this useless piece of machinery. We prepared the engine and after going off shed went to the down yard where we coupled up to a brakevan. The other crews came over to the yard where, as soon as they climbed up into the van, we were under way. With such a light load behind this high-wheeled engine we were soon romping along at a fair rate at knots. After passing Witham I glanced back at the van and saw that a red flag was being displayed so I told the driver and we pulled up alongside Brewham signal box. Being early on a Sunday morning the box was switched out, so we drew forward to the platform at Strap Lane Halt. Here the guard came up and pleaded with us not to go so fast because the brakevan was a rough rider and the occupants were being thrown around all over the place. We didn't exceed 40 mph for the rest of the trip back to Taunton, where an Exeter crew relieved us to take the engine back to its home shed.

No. 2329 *Stephenson* remained at Exeter for some time. It was noticeable that crews never attempted to take more than 18 wagons up Whiteball Bank without assistance when this engine was at the head of the train.

Bristol St Philip's Marsh (SPM) was loaned some former Midland Railway class '2F' 0-6-0 tender engines during the war years. Some of them were relics of the Johnson era and as such were never relied upon for anything more demanding than a trip as far as Weston-super-Mare, Yatton or Wells with a pick-up freight.

On one memorable occasion, late in the war, we found ourselves at the end of the platform at Taunton waiting to relieve the crew of the Lostwithiel to Wood Lane milk train. To our surprise the train rolled in behind a LNER 'O1' class 2-8-0 freight engine, a type with which we were totally unfamiliar. George Smith and I climbed on board and took a quick look around. While I discovered how the injectors worked George had to find out about lubrication, the reversing mechanism and the horizontally mounted pull-out regulator. With all the wartime propaganda slogans fresh in our minds that encouraged all of us to 'Go to it!', etc., this was no time to insist on a proper training course. The driver we were relieving was explaining to George how the vacuum brake worked

'Hall' class 4-6-0 No. 4908 *Broome Hall* with chargehand Fred Rowlands and two lady engine cleaners, recruited during wartime, seen posing for the camera at Taunton on 11th July, 1946.

John Alves

Newport Ebbw Junction-allocated '28XX' class 2-8-0 No. 2894 with a down class 'H' goods train at Whitehall, Taunton, on the goods loop with the locomotive shed to the left, 18th January, 1947.

Roger Venning

when the guard came up and advised us that the train consisted of 20 loaded milk wagons and a brake van making for a load of 400 tons. The signals were clear and as soon as the guard had returned to his van and given us a green light we were on our way. George groped around in the cab roof blew the whistle and then gently pulled the regulator open. The engine responded by gliding smoothly forward and in no time at all the reversing screw was being wound back to shorten the cut-off. The engine was numbered in the '38XX' series, and I remember clearly how different I found this engine to be from our own '38XX' class 2-8-0s and wondered at the time just how this engine had come to wander so far from home.

As this engine picked up speed it appeared that this foreign machine was a very willing mount. There was not a bump, rattle, shake or vibration of any description and the riding was as comfortable as if we were in a coach. I began to fire the engine in the same manner as I would a Great Western locomotive and it appeared to steam freely with the usual 'haycock' fire. We were now speeding along at about 50 mph with the engine showing no outward signs of distress at having to hurry with a class 'D' headcode, express milk train.

With the cut-off wound back to about 25 per cent the engine just took everything in its stride as we struck out across the moors to Athelney and Langport. It continued to steam freely and run smoothly as we began the climb towards Somerton tunnel and then romped along over the level sections to Castle Cary. As we began the climb to Brewham George lengthened the cut-off to about 30 per cent but once we were over the top he shut the regulator and we coasted down through Witham and along the section past Woodlands signal box. During the final miles of our trip to Westbury along the Frome avoiding line and down over Fairwood troughs I began to wish that I was going all the way to London with this engine. When our relief stepped up I was a bit reluctant to get off, because this engine had performed so perfectly at a time when we had become used to the rundown condition of our own Great Western fleet. Many would not think it possible for a dyed in the wool GW man to find anything good in the locomotives of another company but praise must be given where it is due!

As the war dragged on the train services became increasingly disrupted. 'Double-home' working became impracticable. In fact it would be fair to say that this sort of working largely ceased in the West of England except for the 'Salop' men who continued to work the North to West services between Shrewsbury and Newton Abbot. They were pleased to be able to continue working these diagrams as it enabled them to retain their connections with their Devonshire counterparts which, in turn, ensured them a regular supply of rabbits and dairy farm produce to supplement their meagre wartime food ration. During this period the 'Salop' crews had their own regular engine, No. 5064 *Bishops Castle*, which retained its firehole flap because it was never out during the hours of darkness. This saved the fireman the extra work of shutting the firehole doors between rounds of firing.

I think that the only other trains that ran with regular crews during this period were the branch freight services. The main line freight services ran with any crews which were available and a number of locations on the rail network became Relief Control points where crews would report for orders. Such a point was established in the yard master's office at Taunton and two drivers, Percy Pope ('Panicky Percy') and Philip Sweet, together with Ned Widgery, a former chargeman cleaner, were temporarily promoted to the rank of controller for the duration of the war.

To find enough crews to work all the additional wartime traffic a lot of the branch staff were temporarily transferred to main line sheds. Two such drivers that I can remember coming to Taunton were Alf Williams from St Ives and Bert Sanders from Barnstaple.

Our two crack freight trains on the night shift, which were always given priority over other traffic, were the 9.55 pm Bristol, West Depot to Laira and the 10.55 pm West Depot to Hackney Yard. Even the manning of these important services became subject to the relief controllers with crews signing on at the shed and then walking out to the yard to receive orders as to which train they were to relieve.

Bert Sanders signing on one night at 10.00 pm found himself ordered to relieve the crew of the 9.55 pm West Depot to Hackney which he would work all the way to Newton Abbot. The train was known to us as a 'hard hitter' running under 'C' class headcode with at least 25 per cent of the vans in the train being vacuum-fitted and connected next to the engine. When the train ran in on the down main line Bert and his fireman relieved the Bristol crew close to Taunton West Station signal box and were on their way without undue delay. Bert, however, had led something of a sheltered life at Barnstaple and jogged along quietly to Wellington where he stopped for a banker up to Whiteball. Once he was over the summit he should have run down the other side as fast as the speed limit for 4-wheeled wagons permitted but instead he shut off steam and told his fireman to wind on the handbrake, treating the train as if it were an unfitted goods. He was quite surprised to find that the distant signal for Cullompton was against him and the signal was lowered for him to go into the platform road where they stopped.

After a wait of about 15 minutes the main line signals were lowered and with a roar and a clatter another freight train went huffling past. 'By golly', said Bert to his fireman, 'He ai'nt half tearing on'. 'Yes', replied his fireman, 'But we were supposed to be an hour in front him. That's the 10.55 pm West Depot!' Bert never did get the hang of running fitted freight trains fast.

One evening in 1943 I signed on at 7.00 on a Sunday evening as Control Relief and was sent straight away to the down main platform in Taunton station to relieve a train of loco coal destined for Laira Shed. This train had a high priority attached to it, carrying an 'H' class headcode and the reporting number 245. Laira depot had become desperately short of coal and the train had special orders to be kept running at all costs. A '38XX' class 2-8-0 steamed in and we relieved a Bristol crew. We didn't hang around but the signals were clear only as far as West Junction signal box where we were stopped again. Here George, my driver, gave me a notice to take to the signalman and as I crossed the tracks to the signal box I could see that he was about pull off the points to put us into the loop. I showed him the 'special orders' notice for this train which he then verified by telephoning Control. On receiving confirmation of our priority he started hammering away on his block instruments and we were away in no time leaving a very puzzled signalman examining his train notices in case he had overlooked any other special workings. We enjoyed an uninterrupted run to Newton Abbot were the load was split into two manageable trains for working over the South Devon banks.

I experienced a similar run when firing to Bill Selway. We had signed on duty at 2.45 am and were sent to relieve a down freight at about 5.31 am. This was a train of petrol tanks bound for Exeter. This time we were unaware of the priority attached to this train, until we found all the other trains held up in loops and sidings while we ran non-stop to Exeter Riverside Yard in what seemed no time at all. I had run the fire down and when the shunter cut us off we went straight to shed and disposed of the engine. We then went over to the cabin and having had a wash and a cup of tea began to eat our grub. We then reported to the foreman who asked Bill what time we had come on duty to which Bill replied 2.45. The foreman then enquired, 'Yesterday afternoon or this morning?' Bill replied, 'No this morning!', but the foreman didn't believe us and told us to make our way home to Taunton 'on the cushions' where we signed off at about 10.45 am.

Percy Pope was not labelled as 'Panicky Percy' for nothing. He always doubted his own judgement and was frequently harassed by Bristol men looking for a quick return home. The story goes that at about 4.00 one morning Percy was taking stock of the approaching trains and was trying to assess how he could deploy the sets of men available to him. He improvised a diagram using his tea tin to represent a set of Newton Abbot men he would relieve off an up train to man an expected down service. His milk bottle came to represent a Taunton crew and his box of matches represented a Bristol crew, and so on. Percy had worked it all out very carefully, and he appeared satisfied at having resolved a rather tricky situation until someone came in and picked up his box of matches to light a cigarette. Percy returned to look at his diagram and saw that his box of matches had vanished. 'Bugger it', he said, 'That's a set of Bristol men I've lost'.

The double-framed 2-6-0 tender engines of the '26XX' or 'Aberdare' class were never very popular with any crew who had to work them. Fortunately by the time my footplate career had begun they were becoming to be seen less frequently in the West Country. I remember most of them as swaying old heaps of scrap iron. They were one of the few Great Western locomotives to be fitted with a steam reversing mechanism. The reversing lever was a small piece of steel about 2 in. long by ½ in. thick, secured to the cab side by a pivot bolt. The indicator, which was supposed to show the position of cut-off, was a vertical slotted calibrated gauge bolted to the backhead of the boiler. A pointer at the end of a rod indicated the cut-off that had been selected, but in reality the linkage for the indicator was usually so slack that it invariably bobbed up and down between the mid-gear position and the top of the gauge when you were travelling forward. Any attempt to set the engine in any particular cut-off position was next to impossible.

However, there are always exceptions to the rule and in late July 1943 I found myself signing on at 2.00 pm for Control Relief with a driver called Bert Ellard. Bert was a likeable man with an easy-going disposition and we had not been in

'Aberdare' class 2-6-2 No. 2642, a Newport Ebbw Junction engine, at Gloucester (Horton Road) Shed in 1946.   *Robert Franklin/Roger Venning Collection*

the cabin long before the controller told us to go over to the up goods loop and relieve the crew of a train from Hackney Yard to Bordesley, which we would take as far as Westbury. It consisted of about 50 empty wagons, and my heart sank when I saw at its head 'Aberdare' class 2-6-0, No. 2648. I could see that Bill was none too pleased with what had been provided for this job. As soon as we had relieved the Exeter crew we drew forward to the water column and topped up the old ROD tender with which this engine was paired, and then shovelled some coal forward. When we were ready the guard went back to his van and as soon as the signals cleared we were on our way. As we came off the loop it was evident that this 'Aberdare' was something different. It didn't rattle and it rode very smoothly. What is more, the cut-off pointer appeared to be giving a steady indication of the cut- off Bill had selected. On the steady climb to Somerton tunnel it steamed well and as we got to grips with Brewham it dug its heels in and we came over the top in fine style. Drifting down towards Witham. we saw that the distant was on and as we slowed down further we saw that we were being put into the loop. We stopped and a Westbury driver came over from a train standing in the down loop to say that Control had ordered us to change over.

He then took charge of our 'Aberdare' and we went over to his engine to relieve the fireman who told me that the engine was in trouble for steam. The engine was a '28XX' class 2-8-0 and by coincidence its number was 2846, a variation on the number of the engine we had just left. We waited in the loop for about half an hour before the signals were lowered; having been warned by the fireman about the condition of this engine I soon got the long pricker down off the tool rack in the tender and attempted to clean the fire. Each time I heaved on the long pricker I heard a horrible rasping sound as the tip of this fire iron slid across a bed of solid clinker that appeared to cover the entire grate. In desperation I put the blower on full and hoped that we would be able, to make some steam with the fire that was burning on top of the clinker. During the period spent in the down loop at Witham I managed to get the pressure up to 200 psi and filled the boiler. When we pulled out onto the main line I kept the blower going and fed coal to any part of the grate where it would burn. The train consisted of about 50 loaded wagons which had originated in Banbury and it was soon evident that I was fighting a losing battle on the three mile climb up to Brewham. Having started from Witham with a full head of steam and a boiler full of water we were down to 140 psi and one inch of water in the gauge when we passed through Strap Lane Halt. We rolled down through Bruton with steam shut off and over the next quarter of an hour I managed to fill the boiler and get the pressure back up to 200 psi. Bert was hoping to be put in the loop at Castle Cary where we could have put in some more work on the fire but as we approached all the signals were off. Working the engine with the regulator only ⅓ open and the cut-off adjusted as short as it was possible, we were able to keep moving on the generally falling grades of the Somerton route. When we hit the level section across the moors from Curry Rivel Junction the weight of the train took its toll and we were forced to stop for a blow up. Bert phoned ahead from Athelney box that the engine could go no further than Taunton. As soon as we had rallied the boiler we struggled on to the East Yard where we came off the train and went to shed with very little pressure on the gauge . We left the engine on the servicing pit for the firedroppers to tend to.

Another gang of shed labourers was continuously engaged in coaling engines from the coal stage at Taunton Shed. This was always heavy and dirty work, but during these wartime years the job was frequently made worse by the fact that locomotive coal was frequently delivered in former colliery private owner wagons. This was caused by the shortage of wagons but the men on the coal stage hated them because the floors of the wagons were very uneven and difficult to shovel from. During peacetime these wagons had been returned to the colliery empty but now they went back filled with pit props or sometimes they were commandeered by the Ministry of Food for transporting sugar beet.

0-6-0PT No. 5406 with an auto-trailer waits in Forty Steps carriage sidings, before pulling forward into Taunton's platform 7 with the 11.55 am 'All stations' to Castle Cary on 17th December, 1946.

Roger Venning

Chapter Six

Incidents and Accidents

By 1944 I had risen through the links and had become regular fireman to George Smith in the Top Goods Link. Curiously enough one of our turns in this link was a branch passenger service, requiring us to sign on at 5.00 am and be ready to leave shed at 5.45 with an auto-fitted tank engine. At this time the engine was usually '54XX' 0-6-0PT No. 5412 and we were allowed an additional 30 minutes to couple up to the auto-coach. This was no sinecure as besides the usual coupling hook, vacuum brake hose and train heating pipe there was also the regulator operating rod and whistle cord. Our train formed the 6.20 am service to Bridgwater, arriving at 6.40. Here the train then crossed over from the up to the down platform and became the 6.55 am from Bridgwater to Taunton where it arrived at 7.10. We took water here before we departed again, forming the 7.20 am service from Taunton to Venn Cross (on the Barnstaple branch) where we arrived at 7.50 am.

From Bridgwater the fireman was alone on the footplate because the driver occupied the leading end of the auto-coach which the engine would now propel. It was a busy time for the fireman who, besides having to carry out all his normal duties of maintaining the fire and water level in the boiler, was also required to operate the reversing gear to adjust the cut-off, maintain the vacuum in the brake mechanism and ensure that the hydrostatic lubricator remained operating properly. Also, when the auto-coach was being propelled on a single line the fireman had to collect and surrender the token and ensure that he had the correct token in his possession at all times.

This service crossed over from down to up lines at Venn Cross and almost immediately returned to Taunton where it arrived at about 8.30. Filling the tank again we then set off again as the 8.48 am service to Castle Cary, running via Durston and calling at all stations *en route*. When we arrived at Castle Cary at 9.47 we would take water again from the end of the up platform, before crossing over to the down siding to await the arrival of a Bristol to Weymouth service with which we formed a connection. We could now enjoy our first break since signing on nearly five hours before. We would brew a can of tea, which would be drunk with some relish, and at the same time enjoy a few sandwiches that my dear wife had been able to put together from the meagre wartime rations.

The Bristol-Weymouth service arrived at Castle Cary about 10.05 and we left on the last leg of the journey home from the down platform with the 10.18 am departure for Taunton, arriving at 11.15. When all the passengers had left, we would shunt the trailer into the short siding at the east end between the up and down main lines, which was always referred to as the engine spur; its next working was the 3.50 pm service back to Castle Cary. By the time we got back to shed it would be about 12.15 pm and with 15 minutes allowed for engine disposal we usually hoped that we would be permitted to sign off early. The problem for us was that at this stage of the war there was a severe shortage of men and during the remaining half-hour of our shift the foreman would order

'45XX' class 2-6-2T No. 5571 arrives at Taunton with a train from Yeovil on 14th May, 1936. East
Loop signal box can just be seen in the background.   *M. Yarwood*

A view looking east of Brewham signal box in 1957.   *C.R. Potts Collection*

us to fetch the loco coal from No. 4 road in the West Yard. This situation arose because it was impossible to find any space in which to stable wagons of coal on shed. This additional work was never written onto our duty roster, we resented it after such a busy turn and we usually went to the cabin and waited for the foreman's instructions.

It transpired on one day after we had worked this turn that we arrived back at the shed at about 12.20 pm. Having locked up the engine I went to the cabin to have a wash and George followed close on my heels. Bert Vinnicombe, the day-shift foreman soon came looking for us but as soon as he had opened the door George engaged him in a conversation about mileage payments. At that time an agreement existed whereby we would be paid a day's pay for working 140 miles and any excess would be remunerated at a rate of 1 hour's pay for every additional 15 miles worked.

George remarked, 'Bert, do you remember the time when the Union was fighting for 120 miles a day for a day's pay?' Bert took the bait, 'Oh yes', he said, 'I was on the sectional council at Landore at the time and fought tooth and nail for it'.

'Right', said George. 'We've just done 124 miles and 44 chains. How about letting us sign off?'

'Down and fetch the coal George' said Bert, and marched swiftly out of the cabin. Bert was not going to be caught like that again and the rest of the week he was out at the top of the disposal siding waiting for us.

While still in the Top Goods Link we found ourselves working the 2.30 pm to Minehead which, when it returned to Taunton, became the 5.48 pm to Yeovil. This incident occurred when we were on the last leg of the journey with 2-6-2 'Small Prairie Tank' No. 5571 on a service that left Yeovil (Pen Mill) at about 8.00 pm for Taunton. As we approached Martock, George shut the regulator in preparation to stop when there was a tremendous clatter down between the frames and the reversing lever began to vibrate alarmingly. Momentum was sufficient to carry the train into Martock, where we lit a couple of flare lamps and climbed down from the footplate to inspect the damage. We found that the right-hand valve spindle knuckle joint had partly come out where it connected to the rocking arm, allowing it to make contact with the tyre of the leading coupled wheel, where it had become hopelessly wedged. Being the smaller of the two of us I had to squeeze into the space between the left-hand sandbox and the boiler to disconnect the right-hand inside connection of the rocking arm as well as the front end of the extension rod. Leaving this rod to ride on the leading axle, we were prepared to leave Martock and get the train to Taunton on one cylinder but, unknown to us, the signalman had phoned Yeovil (Pen Mill) for assistance. This soon arrived in the form of a '57XX' 0-6-0PT which was to have taken up banking duties at Castle Cary. We had no further difficulties in getting back to Taunton from where the pannier tank departed to begin its shift on Brewham Bank.

Footplatemen's propensity for drinking when working on steam locomotives was well known, they worked hard in a hot environment, perspired freely and drank large quantities to replace the body fluid they lost. Some had their thirst satisfied with numerous cans of tea and would have a 'brew up' whenever a break occurred. Many firemen would make a 'bee line' for the refreshment kiosk on No. 1 platform at Taunton station as soon as they pulled in. Many

GWR Mogul No. 7314 with the 2.30 pm Taunton to Barnstaple (Victoria Road) train leaving Norton Fitzwarren on 13th September, 1947.   *Roger Venning*

A fine view of Venn Cross station in 1924.   *British Rail*

jumped off before the train had halted and dashed to the kiosk carrying their billy can by the handle with the tea leaves already in it. The attendant at the kiosk would always oblige by filling it with clean boiling water, and then the fireman would rejoin his driver on the footplate. To make sure the brew was perfectly mixed many fireman would swing the can by the handle. One fireman was swinging it around high over his shoulder when the handle broke sending the contents cascading over the side of a carriage. Somewhat crestfallen he returned to the footplate clutching just the wire handle!

Some men preferred stronger liquid and all the best 'watering holes' were well known. One such place was the goods shed at Wiveliscombe which Messrs Arnold and Hancock supplied with a gallon of cider in a stone jar on a daily basis, as a sign of their satisfaction with the service that the railway gave them. The contents were shared out among the staff and there was always some for the crew of the daily pick-up goods train. A particularly greedy driver called Harry could not be satisfied with just one glass and regularly took more than his fair share. On one occasion he managed to empty the jar completely. This behaviour did not meet with the approval of the goods shed staff and so they decided to set a trap for him. They secreted the next day's supply in another hiding place and left out the previous day's jar, containing only a small amount of cider laced with a near lethal dose of Epsom Salts. As soon as the goods train arrived at Wiveliscombe the next morning Harry headed for the cabin leaving his fireman to do all the shunting. Needless to say he did not leave the cabin until he had emptied the jar and had to be summoned back to the footplate by several blasts on the engine's whistle. The load that day was fairly light and the fireman became surprised when he noticed that Harry had the regulator wide open on the climb to Venn Cross. As soon as they drew up at the station platform Harry already had his braces undone and made a mad dash to the toilets from which he did not re-emerge for at least 20 minutes. Harry then only took a few steps back towards the engine before he turned on his heels and fled back to the toilet.

When Harry recovered his composure the train went on to Morebath and all the other stations where they shunted the goods traffic. The fireman commented that his driver's timekeeping on some of those long remote sections of line was quite remarkable that day, as if Harry had an appointment to keep. Needless to say he never touched the cider jar again.

Comparatively late in the war it was decided that it was important for footplate crews from the Great Western Shed at Exeter and the Southern Railway men from Exmouth Junction Shed to have route knowledge of each other's lines to Plymouth and from Yeovil to Exeter in case operating emergencies ever occurred. The Western men found themselves undertaking some return workings from Exeter to Plymouth via Okehampton and Tavistock. The Southern men found themselves working the 10. 15 am from Exeter (St Davids) to Taunton, then the 2.05 pm from Taunton to Yeovil returning with the 4.05 Yeovil to Taunton. They finally returned to Exeter with the 6.20 pm service from Taunton. The first engine crew would be relieved at Yeovil Town by another Exeter crew who had travelled via Honiton and Crewkerne and they would in turn work back to Exeter along the Southern route.

Taunton men who worked the 7.20 am stopping train to Exeter would pilot the Exmouth Junction crew to Taunton with the 10. 15 am service from Exeter, and the Taunton crew whose turn it was to work the 2.05 pm Taunton to Yeovil piloted the Southern crews to Yeovil and back. The Taunton men booked to work the 6.20 pm Taunton to Exeter would pilot the Exmouth Junction men back to Exeter and then work on to Newton Abbot with the 8.45 pm stopping service, returning with the 9.35 pm Penzance to Paddington Sleeping Car train to Taunton. On one occasion George Smith and I had done our duty by the Southern crew and were due to relieve an Exeter crew at 7.30 pm, when they arrived with a stopping service from Paignton, and use this engine for the 8.45 pm stopping service to Newton Abbot. In ran the service from Paignton behind '51XX' class 2-6-2T No. 5132 with a big end knocking badly. George said he would take the engine to shed and have a fitter look at it. Fortunately the fitter who came to inspect the engine was Cyril Luscombe whom we knew quite well. He produced a set of feeler gauges to measure the clearance in thousandth's parts of an inch whereupon I remarked, 'I think that you will get the whole lot, handle and all in there Cyril'. On removing the large cap nut on the crank pin he found I was right! Harry Vernon, the late turn foreman, was not at all amused as his quiet evening was disturbed while he found us a fresh engine in the form of an Exeter '43XX' class 2-6-0.

An incident, in which fortunately I was not in any way involved, occurred when I had joined the No. 1 Passenger Link at Taunton in 1945-46 and served as a timely reminder to us all. A set of Bristol men were working a mid-morning semi-fast passenger train to Newton Abbot. On this particular day they were coasting towards Cowley Bridge Junction on the outskirts of Exeter when a full brake application was made and the train came to an abrupt halt. Neither the driver nor the fireman had applied the brake and couldn't understand what had happened. However the driver sent the fireman down to uncouple the vacuum hose between the engine and the first coach and put the hose on the tender plug so that he could test the vacuum brake on both the engine and the tender. This he found to be in order so the fireman reconnected the pipes and the driver tried to create a vacuum in the train pipe. This he couldn't achieve and so the fireman walked back along the length of the 6-coach train looking for a massive leak. He reached the last coach and was surprised to find that the vacuum pipe was dangling free. He immediately assumed that the hose had jumped off its parking plug and so, inserting the securing split pin, he walked back to the engine. The guard was looking out of his window and the fireman told him what had happened and also what he had done to cure the assumed fault. When the fireman got back up onto the footplate he relayed the same information to the driver who then created a vacuum and drove the train into Exeter St David's station.

The fireman had failed to make a basic observation in such a situation by not checking that the tail lamp was in position. Meanwhile the signalman at Cowley Bridge Junction signal box had advised Stoke Canon signal box that the last train had passed the box without a tail lamp. A 'Vanfit' (a vacuum fitted 4-wheeled van) was discovered on its side in the field adjacent to the railway. This van which had been attached to the rear of the Bristol men's train, had jumped off the track, become uncoupled and had ended up in the field.

Vehicles with a wheelbase of less than 10 ft were already banned from class 'A' passenger trains. As a result of this accident trains conveying vehicles of less than 15 ft wheelbase were restricted to 60 mph. The driver and fireman received a registered caution and both them and the guard were suspended from work for two days.

Frome was a sub-shed of Westbury. It kept its own regular engine for working the auto-train to Taunton and from its appearance it is evident that the staff at this shed took great pride in it. On the side frame behind the front buffer beam someone at the shed had proudly painted in white letters the word 'FROME'. I can remember that at some later date a comedian had blackened out the letter 'F' leaving the word 'ROME'. A similar fate befell 'Duke' class 4-4-0 No. 3283 *Comet* which was once seen carrying a chalked in prefix of 'IN' and a similarly marked suffix 'AX') which made the nameplate read 'INCOMETAX'. Without the information that has become available to the current generation of railway enthusiasts, I often wondered why 'Star' class 4-6-0 No. 4007 was named *Swallowfield Park* when engines which were listed numerically on either side of this locomotive carried 'Star' names. I subsequently learned that the engine was originally named *Rising Star*, but for many years I lived with the mistaken belief that it had been renamed after a large house close to Wellington station. I am now informed by Bill Peto of the Great Western Society that *Swallowfield Park* was in fact the residence of the Russell family, who had long associations with the Great Western Railway from its inception and that this grand house is situated near Reading.

Around this time Westbury Shed had been allocated 'Saint' class 4-6-0 No. 2928 *Saint Sebastian*. By this time it was a well worn specimen of the class and somehow Westbury was able to contrive to use it on passenger diagrams where its own men had minimum contact with it! We took it over at Bristol (Temple Meads) when it arrived with the 7.40 am service from Frome and it was noticeable just how glad the Westbury crew were to hand it over to us. We then used it to work the 9.15 am stopping train to Taunton for which it was singularly unsuitable on account of its big wheels. You didn't have to travel very far before you noticed the roughness of the ride due to the wear in the back axleboxes. The thump of the hammerblow sent shockwaves up through the soles of your boots, the like of which had to be experienced to be believed.

I had very little experience with the '29XX' 'Saint' class but was interested to see No. 2935 *Caynham Court* whenever I was as Bath Road Shed at Bristol. This particular engine had been experimentally fitted with rotary cam poppet valve gear and new cylinders in May 1931. It seemed to lead a sheltered life working on Swindon to Bristol passenger services and, although I never had the opportunity to work on the engine, I recall the Working Timetable for the Bristol area made a specific mention of this particular locomotive. This stated that the maximum load that No. 2935 was permitted to haul up Filton Bank was two coaches less than other members of the '29XX' class.

In March 1945 a serious accident occurred near Creech St Michael as the result of a signalman's negligence. The 11.50 pm Paddington to Penzance overnight passenger service, the 'Down Owl', was allowed to enter the occupied block section between Cogload Junction and Creech St Michael where it collided with

In a sorry state, 'Castle' class No. 5050 *Earl of St Germans* is seen at Taunton Shed on 17th March, 1945, with front-end damage, a result of the accident when it crashed into the rear of a down goods train near Creech St Michael after an oversight by the Cogload signalman.

Pursey Short

the rear of a Bristol to Taunton freight service. I have no clear personal recollection of this accident but my friend and fellow fireman Bob Chudleigh related the circumstances of this incident to me.

The signalman at Cogload Junction box accepted a goods train on the down line from Durston and sent it forward to Creech Junction on the down relief line under clear signals. For some undiscovered reason the signalman forgot to replace his signals to danger after the passing of the goods train. He then accepted the 11.50 pm Paddington to Penzance passenger train from Durston which very soon passed his box under clear signals before he realised he had not received 'Train out of section' from Creech for the previous goods train. By not having replaced his signals to danger, he had effectively overridden all the safety devices which prevented two trains from being in one section on the same line at the same time! With the additional momentum gained from the steeply falling gradient from Cogload flyover, 'Castle' class No. 5050 *Earl of St Germans* (Laira) caught up and collided with the rear end of the down goods at Creech St Michael, smashing the brake van and several wagons to matchwood. Although the goods train was still moving when the collision occurred it was slowing down to negotiate the points that led into Taunton goods loop and yard.

The Bristol-based guard of the goods train was unfortunately killed and it was said at the time that it was an awful thing for the signalman to have on his conscience. He was removed from the box and put to work as a shunter in one of the yards at Taunton, but later worked as a goods guard until he retired. This accident didn't receive a lot of press coverage at the time because of wartime censorship.

Bob also reminded me that in the late 1940s for two weeks of the year a number of special trains were needed for the pea traffic. This traffic originated at Bridgwater and the peas were taken from here to a canning factory somewhere up country. Bob fired on some of these trips which were always hauled by a '2301' 'Dean Goods' 0-6-0 from Bristol, St Philip's Marsh Shed. They still had five of this class at this time, Nos. 2322, 2340, 2426, 2534 and 2578. The locomotive arrived at Taunton with a goods train from Bristol and Bob and his driver then took the locomotive from shed to Fairwater Yard to pick up the guard's van. The train then ran straight to Bridgwater. At Bridgwater the train would pick up 20 to 30 vans packed with peas which they would take on to Bristol and be relieved by a St Philip's Marsh crew. Bob recalls that these were the only occasions when he fired the 'Dean Goods', which he found would steam well on very little coal, but the cab was very narrow and offered little protection from the weather.

Although 1943 had seen the introduction of the Ministry of Supply 'Austerity' class 2-8-0s, it wasn't until after the war that the Great Western acquired any of them. All the engines that were built in advance of immediate military needs were first placed at the disposal of the LMS, the LNER and the SR. Eventually 81 of these were reallocated to the Great Western, having been used elsewhere before. These engines made less of an impression on me than the US built 'S 160' class 2-8-0s which were so radically different to anything we had seen before. Having become familiar with the LMS '8F' 2-8-0 that were built at Swindon and

'WD' 2-8-0 No. 79232 with a down class 'H' goods train on the main line in September 1947. Victory Siding is on the right and to the left, beyond the fence-posts, is the line to Barnstaple.
Roger Venning

'WD' 2-8-0 No. 77421 with a down class 'K' goods train having just left Victory Siding, 23rd September, 1947.   *Roger Venning*

loaned to the GWR, it would be fair to say that the similarities in design were quite apparent. Many expensive forgings and castings had been replaced by fabricated items and the sophisticated Belpaire boiler was replaced with one having a cheaper round top design.

My first encounter with them was in late 1946 when I signed on with Bill Duke for a Control Relief turn on a Saturday afternoon at about 5.00 pm. We found ourselves being sent to relieve a Newton Abbot to Bordesley freight train which was standing on the up goods loop. The engine appeared to be in an appalling condition, caked in such a thick layer of grime that it was impossible to read the number on the cabsheet. We were required to work the train as far as Westbury, from where it would make its way to its destination via Swindon, Oxford and Banbury which would take the pressure off the congested LMS route north of Bristol. While I filled the tender tank Bill went around with his oil can applying lubrication to piston and valve rod gland trimmings and a more substantial amount to the slidebars. The guard appeared and gave us the load and soon my driver blew the whistle for the road. With the signal lowered and the handbrake released we moved on towards East Junction signal box and out onto the up main line. Here with all the signals clear Bill opened the regulator to the halfway mark and wound the reverser back to about the 30 per cent cut-off mark. This 'Austerity' was now picking up her skirts and proceeding at a respectable pace. Despite its outward appearance this was clearly one of the better members of its class and, although it rattled a fair bit, the ride was quite commendable. I was having to fire from the opposite side of the footplate because this was a left-hand drive engine. It seemed unfastidious to the way it was fired and with the load we had on it steamed well with one injector feeding continously. Apart from having to wait at Castle Cary for a Weymouth to Paddington service to precede us and then into the loop at Witham for a parcels train to overtake us, the run to Westbury was uneventful. Having been relieved on arrival at about 10.00 pm, we collected our kit and made our way to the relief cabin and brewed some fresh tea.

Around about midnight the phone rang and the controller asked for the Taunton men. He told us that there was a Banbury to Exeter freight train for us to relieve and work back to Taunton. It was reported as leaving Trowbridge some time ago and it was expected at Westbury station within the next few minutes. The train hove into view in the darkness behind an old 'Bulldog' class 4-4-0. We were relieving a set of Swindon men and the fireman told me that the engine was steaming freely and presenting no problems. As it was going to be some time before we departed we took water from the column and then I shovelled coal forward from the back of the tender. There was nothing to attach or detach from the train at Westbury and soon we were able to whistle for the road. The engine was No. 3454 *Skylark*, which at that time was based at HFD (Hereford), but the fact that it was many miles away from its home depot had come to mean very little during the war years and we were just glad that we had an engine in reasonably good shape as we pulled out of Westbury. We were soon stopped by signals at Fairwood Junction, where we had to wait for a train of empty milk tanks to proceed in front of us. As soon as this train had cleared Clink Road Junction the signalman set the road for us and once again we pulled

On 17th August, 1956 Mogul No. 6398 derailed at Swimbridge while working the 11.40 am Taunton to Barnstaple goods train after suffering brake failure on the steep gradient from Filleigh. Local inhabitants are out in some force to view the spectacle. A pannier tank is involved in recovery work. *Tony Harvey/Roger Venning Collection*

away. I waved the gauge glass lamp to the guard and I saw his lamp waving back indicating all was in order, and at 1.00 on a Sunday morning we had the road to ourselves. Bill, my driver, must have been feeling either energetic or generous because he came across and took my shovel and told me to sit down in his seat and keep my eyes on the road ahead. With the regulator about half open and the reverser set at 45 per cent we slogged up the last of the 1 in 107 grade to Brewham summit and started to accelerate as we passed through the deserted platforms at Strap Lane Halt. Here Bill handed me back the shovel and I went over to screw the handbrake hard on to arrest our speed on the descent to Bruton. We didn't want any 'hot boxes' in the train and so we just maintained a steady pace on to Castle Cary. As we headed for Somerton the road was still clear ahead and with the sensible progress we were making I wasn't being over taxed to keep the water and the fire well up. The effect of drifting gently down through Langport and across the moors to Athelney was almost soporific. Passing over the water troughs at Cogload I was almost asleep when I had the fright of my life when I saw the twin headlamps of an express train heading straight towards us. The effect of the curve at this point made it appear to be on the same track. I was too frozen with fear to say or do anything and the train thundered past us on my left side going the other way. This was the overnight train from Penzance to Paddington but what was it doing going the wrong way on the down relief? Evidently what had happened was that the Permanent Way Gang had occupation of the up line between Cogload and Durston which resulted in single line working over the down relief/down road between Creech Junction and Durston because there was no crossover facilities at Cogload. Even after we had been relieved at Taunton the shock I experienced at seeing what I took to be a train coming straight towards us remained with me for a long time, and is an experience that I can still vividly recall today.

In late 1945 we had two variations on my link's late shift. One turn involved a return trip to Yeovil leaving Taunton at 2.05 pm, followed by the 5.25 pm to Minehead and back. The second turn was a return working to Minehead, departing Taunton at 2.30 pm and then forming the 5.48 to Yeovil and back. It was for this later working that we had '2251' class 0-6-0 No. 2213 allocated to us and, having prepared the engine, we went off shed and coupled up to our train in the Minehead bay, platform No. 4. We were ready for the guard's signal when along came locomotive inspector Vercoe and immediately reprimanded me for hanging our front headlamp on the bracket over the right-hand buffer.

'You're experienced enough to know the correct headlamp code!', he told me. 'Yes, I know the code alright', I replied; stepping down from the footplate I invited him to join me at the smokebox end of the engine. Here I removed the lamp from the original bracket and asked him how I was to fit it in the prescribed position as there was neither a lamp bracket on the top of the smokebox or on the door. He was astonished that this engine had just returned from Swindon Works without a lamp bracket fitted there. 'O.K.', he said, 'Put it on the middle bracket!' So I tried this and he saw that the step at the bottom of the smokebox door fouled the lamp and prevented it being secured there. He then walked off in disgust and minutes later we left for Minehead. About a week later I saw No. 2213 on shed with a fitter welding a lamp bracket to the top of the smokebox.

'Castle' class 4-6-0 No. 5043 *Earl of Mount Edgcumbe* passes Taunton's Railway Street and enters platform 7 with a Plymouth to Paddington express on 4th May, 1946. *Pursey Short*

'King' class 4-6-0 No. 6004 *King George III* with the 8.30 am Plymouth to Paddington express at Taunton in April 1947. The fireman can be seen pulling coal forward on the tender.

Roger Venning

Chapter Seven

To Paddington and Plymouth

In the years immediately following the end of World War II the track was in need of particular attention. The war effort had exacted a heavy toll on the railway as, in the struggle to keep the system working some maintenance had been deferred indefinitely. During the late 1940s engineers trains were out every Sunday bringing the track back to optimum condition. A certain fireman I know was on the footplate of a permanent way train working in the Somerton area. Movements were infrequent and being a country lad he always kept his eye open for the chance of catching the odd rabbit. During a lengthy period of inactivity on this hot summer day he was roaming around the side of the track chatting with the guard when he saw what he thought was a rabbit dive under a plank of wood lying in the cess. Sure of his luck he enlisted the help of the guard to assist him in catching the 'bunny'. The guard was to lift one end of the plank while he lifted the other and at the given signal he was going to grab the animal. The plank was swiftly raised and the fireman dived forwards to grab what to him was just a flash of fur. Being a hot day the fireman had left his jacket in the cab and had the top of his shirt wide open. The guard recalled that no sooner had the fireman made his dive forward than he was hastily jumping back, ripping off his shirt, kicking off his boots and struggling out of his trousers as if he was doing some sort of rapid and contorted striptease dance. A thin furry object jumped out of the fireman's trousers and vanished in the undergrowth. It was a stoat! When the plank had been lifted and fireman went forward the stoat had leapt straight down the front of his open shirt !

During the immediate post-war period steam coal was also in short supply and a scheme was devised for a number of locomotives to be converted to burn oil. A number of 'Castles', 'Halls' and '28XXs' were modified and to identify the latter class of locomotives they were renumbered in the '48XX' series, the existing '48XX' a class of auto-fitted 0-4-2 tanks being renumbered to '14XX' to avoid confusion.

One of these oil burning '48XX' 2-8-0s was hauling a heavy freight train from Bristol to Newton Abbot. When it arrived at Wellington it was put in the platform road and the signalman told the footplate crew that they would have to wait for two trains to overtake them. Concerned that even with the burner turned down low the safety valves were still blowing off furiously, the fireman decided to turn off the steam supply to the burner. However, when he did this he omitted to turn off the oil supply also and as a consequence the ash pan became flooded with oil. After the two trains had passed the signalman pulled off for the freight train to go. At this point there was a hurried telephone call from the driver to the signalman informing him that the locomotive would have to return to Taunton because they were concerned of the possible consequences of re-lighting the burner with the ash pan flooded with oil. The banker was summoned and it towed the '48XX' back to shed. The irate foreman at Taunton demanded to know what they had done and so the fireman explained, 'Well 'tis like this Guv. Neither my mate nor I had a match to re-light the burner!'

2-8-0 No. 4807 (formerly No. 2848) has been coverted to burn oil, and is seen here waiting for signals at Taunton (East Yard) with the 3.30 am Tavistock Junction to Bristol Goods in July 1947.
Roger Venning

'Castle' class 4-6-0 No. 5039 *Rhuddlan Castle*, which had been converted to burn oil in December 1946, leaves Taunton Shed in preparation to take the 4.35 pm train to Paddington via Bristol in July 1947.   *Roger Venning*

The years from 1946 to 1948 stand out most vividly in my memories of my footplate career. The stereotype image of the footplate was of two men on a highly polished gleaming locomotive with a train of coaches hurtling along at speed. During those two years I became part of that picture but experience had taught me that this only represented about 1 per cent of the routine work of the drivers and firemen in the days of the steam locomotive.

I had eventually worked my way up to become a fireman in the No. 1 Passenger Link where most of our work was on express passenger trains. I had worked hard and had studied with the mutual improvement class and began to feel that I had really arrived. But then to put the cream on the cake I became Fred Mogg's regular fireman. Fred was an expert engineman who not only drove each engine in a most efficient manner, but as a driver really appreciated the effort and skill that I applied to my work. To provide you with an insight into what I mean let me relate this day's work that took place in July 1947.

Our turn of duty was to work the 8.30 am ex-Plymouth (North Road) to Paddington and return with the 4.30 pm Paddington to Plymouth as far as Taunton. We signed on for this job at 10.26 am which gave us 11 minutes to read any late notices, draw an allowance of four ounces of cotton waste from the stores and walk to the station where the train was due to arrive at 10.37 am. Fred was not the sort of driver who would sign on and get to the station at the last minute and today was no exception because we were waiting to take over the engine at least five minutes before it arrived.

In rolled our train behind 'King' class 4-6-0 No. 6019 *King Henry V* and no sooner had it stopped than Fred was up on the footplate putting his food box on the tender behind the water scoop handle. After exchanging a few brief comments with the driver, he would grab the oil feeder and get off the engine on his side to make a quick examination of the bearings and top up any lubrication points that needed filling. He paid particular attention to the oil cups that lubricated the piston glands, valve spindle glands and the slide bars. As he went he checked each of the wheel centres with the back of his hand to make sure that none of them was overheating. He repeated this procedure on the fireman's side, kneeling down to reach the wheel centre where the platform edge got in his way. When he was satisfied that all was well he got back on the footplate and checked that I was happy with how things were.

That day everything was in apple pie order. As soon as the Laira crew had left the footplate I had a quick sweep around with the hand brush and then washed down the footplate with the 'pet-pipe'. I then looked back along the train for the guard to give us the 'right away' with the green flag. As soon as I had this signal I would shout across to Fred who had put the engine in full forward gear. A tug on the whistle chain to warn all concerned that we are about to move off and then Fred opened the regulator gently onto the first valve. I looked forward to observe that all our signals are correctly set; we will cross over from up relief to up main at the first crossover .

As we entered the gentle left-hand curve I notice that all the other signals were lowered and, looking back along the train, I checked that nobody was trying to make a late entry or exit from the carriages, and that the train is following in the prescribed manner. I had shut off the right-hand live steam injector and flipped up the firehole flap when we had been given the 'right away'. The engine accelerated away with the

'King' class 4-6-0 No. 6019 *King Henry V* leaves Taunton with the 8.30 am Plymouth to Paddington express on 27th September, 1947.   *Roger Venning*

bark of the exhaust echoing back and as we passed Taunton East Junction signal box Fred had the cut-off wound back to 40 per cent. Another look ahead to check if the advanced starter was off and then we were able to settle down to business. Fred reduced the cut-off still further to 15 per cent, excess pressure valves on the cylinder heads snapped away like a pack of excited pups, but as he opened the regulator well into the second valve the noise settled down to a steady rhythm and we flew under Bathpool bridge with the speed touching the 60 mph mark.

The ATC bell rang out as we hit the ramp for Creech St Michael up distant signal and things were looking very promising. The safety valves began to sizzle and so I put the exhaust injector on, checking that it was working properly. Now I took the shovel and started ladling coal into the white hot inferno of the firebox. To start my round of firing I aimed a good shovelful to each of the front corners followed by two or three back each side, then two in each back corner finishing with four or five up the middle to maintain the haycock shape to the fire. As we dashed through Creech St Michael Halt I prepared to take water from the troughs that lie between here and Cogload. A quick check on my injector and then across to the driver's side to the water scoop handle where I raised the locking lever. As soon as the ATC bell rings for Cogload's distant signal I wound the scoop right down as far as it would go and waited for us to hit the trough. Keeping my eyes fixed on the tender water level gauge I started to wind up the scoop, taking up the slack in the pins and linkage of the mechanism. The handle became stiff then and more effort was required to raise the blade until it was horizontal, just skimming the trough in the optimum horizontal plane. As the gauge rose to the full mark it was just two complete turns to lift the blade out of the water and then I fixed the handle by pulling the lever down into the locked position.

Back on the shovel I started to build the fire up ready for the climb to Somerton and beyond to Castle Cary and Brewham. We rushed under the Cogload flyover that takes the down road of the original Bristol and Exeter line over the later Somerton 'Cut-Off' and we were bowling along in a shallow cutting at about 70 mph. The next signal to look out for was Athelney. Fred noticed that I had looked up from my labours to spot this signal and he took the opportunity to re-adjust the rate of oil flowing in the sight feed glasses on the hydrostatic lubricator. Eventually he got it regulated to about six small globules of oil per minute in each of the cylinder glasses and one every two minutes in the glass for the regulator valve. I thought to myself just how many other drivers I had fired to had completely neglected this last glass.

As I returned to the shovel again it seemed to me that this was a wonderful way to earn your living. The firing rate was only about 30 lb. per mile and I didn't even have to resort to lifting the flap between each shovelful as we galloped across Sedgemoor on that day. The needle of the boiler pressure gauge seemed to be glued on 250 psi and the exhaust injector sang away merrily as it maintained the water level in the boiler about an inch down from the top nut in the gauge. We rattled over Curry Rivel Junction and then crossed the over River Parrett on the viaduct just west of Langport. We were now climbing towards Somerton tunnel and as we shot through the platforms of Langport East station I wondered why the company had named this station 'East' when it was situated on the northern extremity of the town. A steady rise of 1 in 264 took us through the wayside station of Long Sutton & Pitney and then quickly into

Somerton tunnel. Even in darkness you could always tell when you were about to emerge from this tunnel because the noise coming up from the rails took on a harsher note as the track is laid on a bed of blue lias stone at this point.

Out into the rock cutting, along a short length of level followed by a brief descent we passed Somerton signal box on our right and on a sweeping left-hand curve we sped through Somerton station. We passed under a road bridge and into another deep cutting but quickly we were out onto a viaduct from which we could see a sweep of landscape invisibly marked by the legends of Avalon. Gentle gradients took us climbing to Charlton Mackrell and then descending to Keinton Mandeville where we crossed over the Fosse Way. From here to Alford Halt was a speedway but soon after we passed the box and the sidings on the right that served a wartime MOD depot, the ATC bell rings out for Castle Cary distant signal. Here Fred eased down the regulator in order to comply with the permanent 65 mph speed restriction where the Weymouth line joins us, swinging in from the right soon after we passed under the road bridge.

The modern brick signal box was a grim reminder of the bombing raid of Thursday 3rd September, 1942 in which three were killed and 11 injured. It destroyed the previous box, a shunting engine and numerous wagons.

Once we were through the platforms at Castle Cary the climb to Brewham began. As we approached Wyke signal box the gradient stiffened to 1 in 98 and continued as we climbed under the S&D line and on to Bruton. Looking to our right at this point we could see the S&D station at Cole.

Fred had the regulator ¾ open but as the gradient began to slow us down he lengthened the cut-off first to 20 per cent and then 25 per cent as we roared past the back of Sexey's School and through Bruton station. Climbing all the way at 1 in 93 we curved to the left and passed Sheephouse Crossing. The speed now dropped away to about 45 mph and approaching the site of the signal box at Pinkwood, the exhaust took on a sharper note as we tackled the 1 in 81 through the wooden platforms of Strap Lane Halt. Under the road bridge and on the

A close-up view of the signal box at Castle Cary which replaced an earlier one destroyed by enemy action during World War II.   *Exe-Rail*

right-hand side was Brewham signal box which marked the summit of the climb; from the footplate it was possible to see the track dip down the other side at 1 in 107. Once we were over the top and accelerating down the bank towards Witham, Fred eased down the regulator and wound the cut-off back to 15 per cent. We rattled over the junction at Witham station and sped on towards Woodlands box and then Blatchbridge Junction. Here it was my turn to look ahead for the distant signals, making sure that the right-hand signal was pulled off indicating that we were to run up the Frome avoiding line. If the left-hand one had been off Fred would have to have made a heavy brake application to traverse the junction and then some slow running through Frome station. I called out to Fred 'O.K.' as I saw that the right-hand board had been pulled off for us. Fred kept a sharp look out to check the signals himself when they could be seen from his side of the footplate.

The town of Frome lay on our left as we raced up towards Clink Road Junction and speed rose again as we accelerated downhill on a 1 in 151 gradient towards the water troughs at Fairwood Junction. Here again were another pair of distant signals, the left-hand one for Westbury and the right-hand one for the avoiding line, but Fred made the observations here as I had to go through the drill of taking water from the troughs. Our speed was about 60 mph and I had only 15 seconds to collect 1,800 gallons of water and get the scoop wound up. You had to act smartly here because within a few hundred yards of the end of the trough there was a destructor block set between the rails designed to rip off the mouth of any tender water scoop left dangling, preventing it from damaging the junction point work.

We sped under the bridge carrying the Westbury to Salisbury line and around the back of Westbury Shed. Soon after the ATC bell rang out for Heywood Road Junction where the line from Westbury rejoined us on our left. The track is level for the next six miles and we got into our stride again under the shadow of the Westbury White Horse, romping on towards Edington & Bratton. Despite the level track there was no respite for me as I had been steadily building up the fire for the 18 mile climb to Savernake that began just

Savernake station looking towards Plymouth, a train for the Marlborough branch is in the bay platform. *C.R. Potts Collection*

before Lavington. This was not the steep 1 in 80 of Whiteball or the 1 in 40 of Dainton but the eight miles averaging 1 in 222 to Patney & Chirton required the engine to develop greater power if the train was to run to time, and thus made more work for yours truly on the shovel. As we approached Patney the line from Holt Junction and Devizes joined us on the left running in at a higher level than the West of England main line. At this time there was a train from Bristol along this route worked by a Bath Road crew that we often met when we were in that city. Knowing that from the footplate of their 'Hall' they could look down into our cab I decided to make our job look really easy. I turned on the 'pep-pipe', and sprayed the coal in the tender to dampen down the dust. The fact that this water is being diverted from the boiler feed at this point caused the safety valves to simmer and we showed off by storming up the bank alongside them with the injector on and the firehole doors wide open.

The road from here still climbed through Woodborough, Pewsey and Wootton Rivers but there were some undulations that gave us some relief and speed was maintained in the mid-60s for some time. By now I had been working with Fred long enough to recognise his every move and as we passed Burbage, a small signal box with a siding one mile short of Savernake, he shut the regulator in order to bring our speed down to the regulation 50 mph speed limit without applying the brake for the curve at Grafton East where the Midland & South Western Junction line crossed over our line on a bridge.

Coasting past the old pumping engines at Crofton the water in the boiler had come down to half a glass and with the exhaust injector having cut out when the regulator was closed, I put on the right-hand live steam injector to prevent the safety valves from blowing. The water level would rise slowly as we rolled through Bedwyn and down to Hungerford. The fine judgement that Fred demonstrated by shutting off at Burbage meant that we had let the gradient control the speed of the train without having to touch the brakes all the way to Hungerford. But as we approached this station he opened the regulator and set the cut-off at 15 per cent again and we sailed on down the rest of the gradient through Kintbury, Hamstead Crossing and Enborne Junction, where the line from Winchester joined us from the right. Under another road bridge and we flew through Newbury and on past the station built to serve the racecourse.

It was easier steaming along this stretch of line through Thatcham and Midgham with a gentle descent in our favour until we began to approach Reading. At Aldermaston we got our last opportunity to take water before Paddington and then it was not long before we passed Theale and the small signal box at Calcot. Fred shut the regulator soon after we passed Southcote Junction where the line to Basingstoke joined us from the right. We ran through the platforms at Reading West, over the pointwork of Oxford Road Junction and along the back of Reading Loco Shed but here the ATC siren wailed out because the distant signal for Reading General was at caution. We expected this because we had to run via the platform line to slip two coaches. I had wound the tender handbrake on to keep the speed down to 40 mph, and to hold the tension off the couplings, making it easier for the slip guard to operate the uncoupling handle. Halfway along the platform I released the handbrake and Fred looks back along the train to check that the slip coaches were being left behind us. Seeing that all the signals were clear he gently opened the regulator and without a snatch or hiccup we glided steadily through the crossover and out onto the main line again. Our speed began to build as we ran out of Reading past Kennet Bridge and on to Sonning Cutting.

The last time I added coal to the fire was after we had taken water at Aldermaston and I reckoned that we had enough in the box to get us through to Paddington, from where the engine is due to go for servicing at Old Oak Common.

Although most regular passengers knew the sequence of the station names between Reading and Paddington only the railwaymen remembered the additional landmarks of the signal boxes. After Sonning Cutting came Woodley Bridge and then Twyford West and East boxes. Then came Ruscombe, Shottesbrook and Waltham Siding before Maidenhead, West, Middle and East. Then we crossed the Thames on Brunel's famous flat-arched bridge and continued our rush towards the capital passing through Taplow and Burnham.

Slough and Langley were soon behind us and as we approached Iver I got the long pricker down off the tender and spread the remains of the fire all over the grate. If I maintained the water level in the boiler at about half a glass I would have enough room to keep the safety valves quiet when standing at Paddington by feeding more cold water into the boiler with the live steam injector.

True to form Fred shut off steam for the run into Paddington as we passed Ealing Broadway. I left the fire alone and concentrated on helping Fred by observing the signals which were all colour lights from here. I noticed the number eight displayed in lights on one signal which indicates that we would arrive on Platform 8 at Paddington. Here Fred made his first brake application since leaving Taunton as we came to a stop dead on time. The relieving crew stepped up onto the footplate and we told them that we had no faults to report. We made our way to the canteen on platform 1 where we had a wash before eating our sandwiches.

Our return working to Taunton was the 4.30 pm express for Plymouth and on the occasion I am about to describe the train included a restaurant car and a number of coaches for Kingswear which were detached at Exeter. We were allowed 157 minutes for the 143 miles to our first stop at Taunton where we were due to arrive at 7.07 pm. The locomotive for the return working would be brought to Paddington for us and so we waited on the end of platform 1. At about 4.00 pm a pannier tank puffed in past the Paddington Departure box with a string of coaches that was to be our train. I had just counted 14 behind the engine when a gentleman approached me and asked if we were the footplate crew that was going to work this train. He said that the Old Oak crews had had a 'King' on this job all this week and they had only 12 on and our load today was 14 coaches, equal to 431 tons. Although we didn't know the identity of this gentleman he was obviously someone of importance because he was carrying a cloth-bound copy of the Working Timetable under his arm.

At 4.20 pm the rear of a 4,000 gallon tender came into sight past the Departure box and the gentleman turned to me and said, 'There, I told you it would be a 'King'. I looked at him and said, 'I've never seen a 'King' with such a tall chimney as that!' and he became quite excited as the number plate revealed No. 5035 and then the nameplate *Coity Castle*.

'Star' class 4-6-0 No. 4039 *Queen Matilda* passes Sonning signal box with a down Plymouth express.   *L&GRP*

Express trains await departure from Paddington on 12th March, 1948. *Left:* an unidentified 'Castle' class, *centre*: 'Grange' class No. 6857 *Tudor Grange* and, *right*: 'County' class No. 1005 *County of Devon*.   *British Rail*

Our gentleman said that we would never make Taunton right time and laid a 10 shilling bet before leaving us to board the train. Fred and I got up on the footplate and were reassured to find that the engine had been expertly prepared. The firebox had been well filled and the coal was well burnt through. The Old Oak men got off the engine and the guard came up to give Fred the load. At 4.30 pm with the signals showing green the guard blew his whistle and waved his flag. Fred gently opened the regulator to set us off homeward once more. When the cylinder cocks were shut we began to accelerate away with the ATC bell ringing in quick succession as we passed Old Oak Common, Ealing Broadway, Southall and Slough, but as we were approaching Maidenhead the siren wailed because a distant signal was against us, marking a 15 mph Restriction of Speed where relaying work would begin the next day.

This locomotive was in truly splendid condition but with the load we had behind it needed to be. I settled down to my usual pattern of firing and when the safety valves began to lift shortly before Old Oak Common I had to get the exhaust injector going. This blew out when steam had been shut off for the speed restriction, but as the water was high in the glass I let the safety valves roar thereby making sure that Fred would have plenty of steam to accelerate away. The water level came down to ⅔ of a glass but with the regulator open once more I could set the exhaust injector to work again. I knew that I could leave it running until we came out of Sonning cutting because, unless there were adverse signals, Fred would not close the regulator until he shut off for Reading. I was ready for this when it happened and all I had to do was put on the right-hand injector as he shut the regulator, at the same time opening the supplementary steam valve of the exhaust injector. Leaving the flap up I put the blower on a just a touch so as to clear the smoke and steam from the top of the chimney. We ran through Reading and around the curve to Oxford Road Junction at the mandatory 40 mph, with not a trace of smoke or steam along the top of the boiler. When Fred opened up onto the second valve of the regulator I shut down the blower, the right-hand injector and the supplementary steam valve of the exhaust injector. As the safety valves lifted I opened the firehole flap and began firing again in earnest. The cooling effect of the fresh charge of coal on the grate soon closed the safety valves and I was able to settle down to my usual round of firing. As a result of the lengthy restriction of speed at Maidenhead we were now running six minutes down and I suspected that the gentleman in the train was beginning to think that his 10 bob note was safe in his wallet.

Once we were past Southcote Junction, Fred set the cut-off at 15 per cent and with ¾ regulator I noticed we passed Theale rather more rapidly than usual. At Aldermaston troughs we took our first fill of the tender and soon after we seemed to be making a mad dash through Newbury. This was a superb locomotive and we thrashed on past Enborne Junction, Hamstead Crossing and Kintbury in quick succession but as we approached Hungerford so the effect of the steepening gradient began to make itself felt. Fred increased the cut-off to 20 per cent for the climb past Bedwyn and he left it there until we had come round the curve at Grafton East Junction and cleared the summit at Savernake (Low Level). Despite this spirited climb we had not made up any time and we were

'Castle' class 4-6-0 No. 5027 *Farleigh Castle* with the Minehead-Paddington (Saturdays-only) train passing Pewsey on 9th July, 1938.   *M. Yarwood*

still six minutes down as we began to fly down through Wootton Rivers, Pewsey, Woodborough, Patney & Chirton and Lavington. Our speed along this section was fast enough for the ATC bell to ring like the Taunton church bells on Old Year's Night.

At Heywood Road Junction we carried on down the Westbury avoiding line and as we passed Fairwood Road Junction it was time to take water from the troughs. We were going well again as the beginning of the climb to Brewham started to make itself felt on the rise to Clink Road Junction. I had my head down feeding the fire and I was surprised when Fred shut the regulator causing the exhaust injector to blow out and the safety valves to lift with a roar. I looked up at the signals we were passing and realised that we were being sent in around Frome. I quickly put on the right-hand injector to keep the safety valves quiet and Fred brought our speed down for the 30 mph speed restriction through the station. We were pleased to see that the distant for Blatchbridge Junction was clear and when we got there we saw the reason for our diversion; a freight train standing on the avoiding line by Blatchbridge home signal. We registered our disgust by blowing an insulting code on our whistle as we passed over the junction and then Fred really let rip, lifting the regulator wide open with the cut-off set at 25 per cent. The excess pressure valves on the cylinder ends began to pop away like machine guns but by the time we had climbed to Witham we were back in our steady rhythm again.

Any time we had saved on our downhill dash from Savernake had been lost through our unexpected diversion through Frome and we were still 6 minutes down. Once we were over the top of Brewham, our speed built up to the mid-70s on the descent to Bruton and it stayed there until we approached Castle Cary, where we rattled over the junction pointwork rather faster than the permitted 60 mph. Now we were back on the racetrack with a modern gently graded line laid out for high speed running. Things began to hum on this section and glancing over Fred's shoulder I could see that our speed which had been 72 mph at Keinton Mandeville had increased to 75 mph at Somerton. As we emerged from the tunnel we were doing 78 mph and still accelerating down the long straight that led to Curry Rivel Junction. I kept a good look out for the distant signals as we hurtled through Langport East. With the cut-off set at 15 per cent and the regulator half open, I reflected that we would have been very hard pressed to stop if any signal had suddenly been set against us. As we ran across the moors on the approach to Athelney the speedometer registered a maximum of 88 mph which, with a load of 14 coaches equal to 431 tons, was not a bad performance by the standards of the post-war era.

As we swept under the flyover at Cogload I prepared to take our last dip from the troughs. We passed Bathpool Bridge with the firehole doors wide open and the right-hand injector on. In the distance I could see that the signals were off at Taunton East Junction and that we would be crossing from down main to down relief so that we would run into No. 1 Platform. As we stopped a glance at my watch revealed that it was 7.07 pm on the dot! I was gathering my kit together when the Laira fireman got on and then got off again and walked to the front of the engine. When he came back he asked what train we were as we were carrying the reporting number for the 4.30 ex-Paddington. We couldn't have come all the way with this load as the front doors of the tender were still shut. I assured him that we had come 'all the way' and he said that he wished he had a driver like that!

As Fred and I descended from the footplate the gentleman we had last seen at Paddington came up and presented us with a 10 shilling note, congratulating us warmly on an excellent performance. This for me was PERFECTION!

Just a few weeks after this run with No. 5035 *Coity Castle* I was booked on a Saturday to work the 10.40 am from Taunton to Paddington with   driver Edgar Wade. I was pleased to find that yet again we had this engine because the load today was 13 coaches, two of which would be slipped at Reading. Edgar was a good engineman, and I had fired for him before on runs to Paddington but he differed in several ways to my regular driver, particularly in the way that he approached Savernake. Here we had to slow down to 50 mph under the bridge carrying the Midland & South Western Junction line over the top of us and around to Grafton East Junction. Fred Mogg would shut off steam at Burbage about a mile before reaching the summit at Savernake Low Level so as to let the gradient slow us down to the correct line speed without having to touch the brake. Edgar would keep the steam on to Savernake's home signal before shutting off which necessitated a brake application to reduce our speed to the required limit.

Today all was going well, but when Edgar shut off steam a little earlier than usual on the approach to Savernake there was a distinctive tap, tap, tap, tap from deep down between the frames of the engine. Edgar must have seen the look of apprehension on my face for he immediately said to me, 'I heard that when we left Taunton, didn't you?' When I said 'No' he began to get a bit agitated.

Wolfhall Junction signal box (*right*). In the distance is the bridge that carried the Midland & South Western Junction line over the Great Western main line.   *L&GRP*

As we ran past Wolfhall Junction I saw that Grafton Junction's distant was on. I called them out to Edgar and then when the home signal came in sight in the danger position Edgar applied the brake and we came to a stand. Here Edgar grabbed the oil feeder filled with at least two pints of oil, from the tray over the firehole where it had been keeping warm. He got down from my side of the engine and walked forward along the ballast to a point where he was able to put his hand through a hole in the frame adjacent to the inside big end bearing. I saw him pull it out again quite swiftly and then I was amazed to see him crawl under the engine, between the wheels, to add oil to the reservoir of the inside left-hand big end bearing which was running hot. I made sure that the handbrake was firmly applied and then got down to see if he wanted any help. He showed me the cork that he had just replaced. This cork had been pushed down so hard that it had a dimple in the end indicating that it had been hard up against the restrictor plug. This had stopped the flow of oil to the big end bearing causing it to overheat and melt the white metal anti-friction material. Edgar's treatment was too late to save the big end and once we were back on the footplate we pulled forward as far as the box when the signal was now lowered. Here we told the signalman to tell Reading that we would be wanting a fresh engine and so we pulled forward and stopped again for the signalman to relay this message to the guard in the brake compartment of the slip coach portion. Edgar nursed the engine along from here to ease the knocking from our damaged big end and I had little to do as the engine would be going to shed at Reading and the fire would need to be kept as low as possible. Fortunately the line descends virtually all the way down the Kennet valley and when we eventually arrived at Reading we were relieved by another crew who told us that we were to take the engine that was on east station pilot duty, which turned out to be '43XX' class 2-6-0 No. 6313.

This was a poor substitute for a 'Castle' with such a load but we coupled up and in what seemed no time at all Edgar had the ejector wide open to create a vacuum. I had had little opportunity to pay any real attention to the state of the fire but when I did my heart sank because it was just half a box of very dull to black fire. The guard gave us the 'right away', I turned the blower on full and got the pricker down off the tender and attempted to spread what fire we had more evenly over the grate. I then grabbed the shovel and found that there was just a mish-mash of small coal and rubbish on the front of the tender. Clearly it wasn't anticipated that this engine would be travelling very far. Edgar wasn't going to have any time booked against him and was giving the engine 'the gun' in getting our 11 coaches out of Reading. The regulator was wide open and the reversing lever was set in the 40 per cent cut-off notch. All I could do was shovel coal as fast as possible. No fancy 'haycock' fire now, just keep that roaring furnace fed. I reckoned that each shovelful held about 15 lb. of coal and I was firing these at a rate of about six shovelfuls a minute into the firebox of this hungry brute. Most of the small coal went straight out through the tubes and up the chimney leaving a black plume behind us. There was no time to notice familiar landmarks, I just kept my back bent and my head down and shovelled whatever sort of coal I could find into a firebox that resembled Dante's Inferno. I caught a glimpse of Ealing Broadway and realised that the fire was still no higher than when we had left Reading. The exhaust injector had been on all the way and the boiler water gauge still registered no more than half a glass. What a difference to No. 5035! Anticipating that Edgar would soon be shutting off to run into Paddington I put on the right-hand injector as well and stopped shovelling coal. The palms of my hands were red and sore from the couple of tons of small coal I had shifted during the past 40 minutes, and clearly this engine was incapable of keeping time with such a load. As we ran into No. 8 platform I was glad to see our relief and when we got off the footplate I noticed that the bottom of the smokebox door was red hot and sizzling with the heat.

I went to the wash room and let cold water run over my sore hands they were too painful to attempt applying soap to them straightaway. After a minute or so I found that I could just bear soap on them and then I stripped off to the waist and washed my face, neck, shoulders and arms. After this I felt much better and was soon able to join Edgar in the canteen where I had a cup of tea, ate my sandwiches and was able to reflect more philosophically on the last hour's work.

Thankfully on this occasion there was no back working and we came home as passengers on the next train to Taunton. As we passed Maidenhead Edgar was looking out of the window and said, 'I think we are going to have some rain, there's a dirty black cloud up there?' 'Oh no', I said to Edgar, 'That's the cloud we put up there on our way to Paddington this morning!'

The section of the main line to Plymouth that runs along the sea wall between Dawlish and Teignmouth is a very picturesque setting in fine sunny weather, which has been successfully exploited by generations of railway

'Star' class 4-6-0 No. 4060 *Princess Eugenie* is seen with the down 'North Mail' at Exeter (St David's), the 12.05 am ex-Liverpool and the 12.30 am ex-Manchester express, in March 1947.

Roger Venning

photographers. In winter time it could present an entirely different aspect. The worst weather conditions that could be experienced on the footplate would be encountered when a strong south-easterly gale blew in from the English Channel striking the coast at an angle of 90 degrees. When these conditions prevailed high rolling waves would surge in and break on the sea wall, sending thousands of gallons of salt water vertically into the air to smash down on the railway track, sometimes washing the ballast away or flooding the track if the drainage channels had been allowed to become blocked.

Whatever the weather we were still expected to keep the trains running and to the times published in the timetables. As mentioned in an earlier chapter, in 1944 footplate crews from the GW shed at Exeter began to learn the road to Plymouth via the Southern Railway route that lay through Crediton, Okehampton and Tavistock. Simultaneously the Southern crews from Exmouth Junction Shed began to operate their locomotives over the Great Western route via Newton Abbot and Totnes. The idea was that all Exeter men would have route knowledge if diversions were made in the event of either route becoming blocked.

One morning in October 1946 Fred, my regular driver, and I were working our booked turn of duty with the down 'North Mail'. When we arrived at Exeter (St David's) we were joined on the footplate by a Southern driver, from Exmouth Junction, who introduced himself as Reg Bastin saying that he wanted to travel with us in order to learn the road to Plymouth. We were not detained very long at Exeter and soon after being given the 'right away' we were on our way. Out through Exeter (St Thomas) station and on to Exminster our journey was uneventful, but as I was winding the scoop up from the troughs I shouted to Fred, 'There's a fierce south-easter this morning, there'll be a lot of water on the track at Dawlish. Fred acknowledged my warning and remarked that he would try and keep up a good momentum in order to get us quickly past the worst spots. I had built up a huge fire in the box in anticipation of the impending deluge and soon after passing Dawlish Warren I was able to crowd myself up into the front corner of the cab . As we approached Dawlish I could see that the sea was rough and then I noticed a real purler of a wave surging vertically from the wall about 100 yards in front of us. I had no time to warn the Southern man, who was admiring the view back along the train, before the wave hit us. He was knocked breathless across the footplate and ended up wrapped around the water scoop handle soaked to the skin. After he had recovered his equilibrium he said, 'Bloody hell , I shall have to remember that, we drive our engines on that side!'

I doubt if he ever forgot his christening with about 10 tons of cold brine. From this you can see that route knowledge is just not a matter of signals, junctions and gradients, it's also knowing where and when nature can throw something unpleasant at you.

Perhaps the worst weather conditions I can remember occurred at this period of my career. The long cold winter of 1947 dragged on remorselessly and, coupled with a combination of post-war shortages and the demands imposed by irregular hours, gradually told on our morale. As a senior fireman in the No. 1 link our work rotated around 10 turns which all began at different times of the day or night. For nine weeks we had booked train turns but on the 10th week we

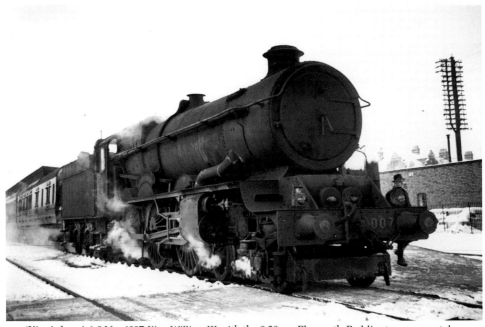

'King' class 4-6-0 No. 6007 *King William III* with the 8.30 am Plymouth-Paddington express takes water at Taunton's platform 7 in bitterly cold conditions in January 1947.   *Roger Venning*

Collett 0-4-2T No. 5812 was the West End shunter on 31st January, 1947 and is seen between duties in Forty Steps carriage sidings on 31st January, 1947.   *Roger Venning*

were rostered as spare, and you would find yourself booked to cover the absence of any fireman in the same link who was either sick or on leave. So it was on Monday 27th January, 1947 that I found myself on the spare turn, and booked out to work the Sunday night 9.50 pm Paddington to Plymouth Sleeper with driver Percy Lowe, which meant signing on duty at 2.40 am.

It was a bitterly cold morning and when I opened the door of the house to set off for work the snow was waist high. I struggled out and had a look at the road and found that it still might be possible to cycle with care so I strapped my grub box to the carrier, and warily made my way up the road keeping to the frozen ruts in the snow. My journey to work which normally took 10 minutes this morning took 25. It was just as well that I set out a bit earlier than usual because I just managed to sign on duty in time. I joined my driver and we made our way to the down platform just as the train ran in at 2.58 am behind 'Castle' class No. 4086 *Builth Castle*. The Bristol driver stopped the engine with the tender opposite the water column and the Bristol fireman told me that Creech troughs were frozen solid and hence he hadn't risked damaging the water scoop. He climbed up on top of the end of the tender while his driver pulled the jib of the water crane around for him. I got hold of the shovel and the coal pick and pulled as much coal forward as I could into the shovelling area. This proved difficult because the coal was frozen and I had to do a lot of work with the pick to separate the lumps. As soon as the tank was filled the Bristol driver pulled the jib back; the fireman told me that the engine was a bit of a rough rider but she was steaming alright and then he got off. I had put the firehole flap up and the blower on a quarter of a turn to keep the fire hot while we were standing in the platform. At 3.04 am I looked back along the platform and saw the guard giving us the green light so shouted 'Right away' to Percy. He lifted the regulator a quarter open while I observed that all the signals were showing green. Percy now opened the regulator to the half-open position, but this proved to be unwise because we were just crossing to the down main and the wheels lost their grip on the cold rails. The wheels spun and the rods clattered and clanked in a dizzy whirl before Percy shut the regulator, gave a pull on the front sanding levers and gently eased the regulator open again. By then we had negotiated the crossover and were on straight track, there was still a trace of sand on the driving wheels allowing them to dig in and accelerate the train smoothly away.

Percy started to wind the reversing screw back to shorten the cut-off making more economic use of the steam being generated in the boiler. I heard the excess pressure valves on the cylinder ends start to pop, Percy left the cut-off adjusted at that position and opened the regulator wide. We roared under Staplegrove Bridge and saw that the signals for Silk Mill Crossing and the distant for Norton Fitzwarren were all clear. Knowing that Percy was a bit heavy handed at times I put the exhaust injector on fine feed, checking the overflow from the lights of the crossing as we flew past. The Bristol fireman was right, this engine rattled a fair bit but was steaming well, appearing to respond well to the fuel I was feeding into firebox. At Wellington we noticed the lights of a PW gang that was at work, keeping the points from freezing, but there wasn't much opportunity for me to look up from my work at this stage on the climb to Whiteball. With 400 tons behind us we were only 20 tons short of the unassisted limit for a

Silk Mill Crossing signal box.   *Exe Rail*

Burlescombe was the nearest station to Whiteball Summit. It is seen here on 7th June, 1921.

Lens of Sutton

'Castle' on the bank but there was no banking engine available on a Sunday night. The coal I had made loose and broken up while we were at Taunton was now being rapidly depleted but Percy, being confident in my abilities, lengthened the cut-off to 35 per cent and our speed did not slacken over Beam Bridge. The water was still over halfway up the gauge and the boiler pressure was steady at 210 psi as we whistled and rushed into the confines of Whiteball tunnel. The only difference we noticed on this dark morning was that it appeared to be warmer in the tunnel. Emerging from the western portal and breasting the summit of the bank it was time to shut the exhaust injector. The feed having been set fine soon after we left Taunton had ensured that pressure would be maintained on the climb at the expense of the water level in the boiler. As we passed Whiteball box I crossed the footplate and turned on the live steam injector, opening the blower a quarter of a turn to maintain the air flow through what was becoming a rather dirty fire.

Percy eased down the regulator for the descent through Burlescombe and Sampford Peverell and even with a substantial accumulation of clinker in the firebed the pressure and the water level began to rise again. As we rolled downhill under light steam I was able to get a bit of coal pulled forward with the coal pick . I could not get up into the tender as this was too dangerous along this stretch of line. When we approached Tiverton Junction it was time to start firing again, but the supply of coal I had pulled forward was enough to get us to Exeter where we arrived at 3.46 am. We had five minutes station time here which was sufficient for me to get up into the tender and pull the best part of 10 cwt of coal forward. During this time Percy went around the engine with the oil can, not having time to do this at Taunton during the changeover. It was not possible for us to take water at Exeter without cutting off and going to into the South Devon Sidings, but there was enough in the tender to get us to Newton Abbot. Being concerned about the state of the fire I got the chisel bar down off the fire iron rack on the tender and attempted to break up as much of the clinker as I could in the time available.

At 3.51 am station work was completed and the guard gave us the 'Right away'. Having had the small ejector on since coming to a rest Percy needed only to open the regulator and soon we were passing over the up and down main line of the Southern Railway which curved away sharply to our left and climbed at 1 in 37 to Exeter Central station. We barked away past Exeter West box , over the River Exe and along the embankment towards Exeter (St Thomas). I had shut off the right-hand injector before I had attacked the fire with the chisel bar back during our stop in Exeter and had shut the blower as we moved off. I had kept the fire hot by keeping the flap up, except when using the chisel bar, and now I started to feed the coal to the brightest parts of the box. Considering that the engine had come from Paddington via Bristol the steaming was still tolerably good and I was able to put on my exhaust injector as we rushed through a deserted St Thomas station and on to City Basin Junction. Approaching Exminster a decision had to be made as whether or not to attempt taking water from the troughs. As we passed the marker lamp I wound down the handle of the scoop and heard the rattle of ice being thrown up from the troughs but this went quickly and then we began to pick up water. Clearly the

Tiverton Junction looking towards Plymouth in 1934.   *British Rail*

'Hall' class 4-6-0 No. 4971 *Stanway Hall* heads a westbound goods train, it is seen approaching Tiverton Junction on 15th July, 1958. The Hemyock branch curves away to the right.

H.C. Casserley

proximity of these troughs to the sea created slightly milder conditions which prevented them from freezing solid. With the water problem solved, we ran without further incident to stop at Newton Abbot at 4.25 am.

Here we were joined by an assisting engine in the form of 'Bulldog' class No. 3383 (it had carried the name *Ilfracombe* until 1930). I got down from our footplate and coupled up the tender of this engine to the front of ours. A convention existed at the time that the fireman of the assisting engine would uncouple when we arrived at Plymouth (North Road). I rejoined Percy on the footplate who soon had the 4-cone ejector on to create a vacuum and then with a green light from our guard, a blast on our whistle, we were away on the final leg of our journey at 4.32 am. Accelerating in fine style out to Aller Junction we swung around to the right and started to climb towards Stoneycombe's signal box and then past the deserted quarry buildings. By the time we got to the steepest part of the bank we were down to 15 mph with both engines blasting away flat out. Once we were through the tunnel and past Dainton signal box we started to drop down to Totnes. I began to think that the driver of the assisting engine was taking a bit of a risk as we swept around reverse curves rather faster then usual but I could only assume that he knew what he was doing. We sped through Totnes and immediately got stuck into the 1 in 60 climb towards Tigley signal box and I fired what coal I had left on the front end of the tender. Between Tigley and Marley tunnel I brought the pricker down off the tender to feel what the state of the firebed was. All I could feel was the rasp of the tip of the pricker as it scraped at the bed of clinker that covered the grate. I decided to keep the fire up to the same level because there was not that much fuel on top of the clinker. I put the blower on a quarter of a turn as we entered the single bore of Marley tunnel as, with an engine in front of us, there was an increased chance of a blow back through the firehole.

Soon we were passing through Brent station and began the last short climb to Wrangaton. Once we were through the 65 yds-long tunnel here it was downhill past Bittaford Halt and Ivybridge. A curving viaduct brought us into Cornwood and then Hemerdon signal box which marked the beginning of the steep descent to Plympton. Here again I felt the speed to be excessive and looking forward I could see that sparks were flying from the Pilot engine's driving and tender wheels. I went across and told Percy who immediately took action and applied our brakes which brought the speed of the train down to an appropriate level.

Having run through Plympton Percy opened the large 4-cone ejector releasing the brakes and we rolled on through the yard at Tavistock Junction at a time when the up and down side shunters had just begun their morning's work. We ran under light steam beside the River Plym and under the road bridge past Laira signal box, where the regulator had to be opened for the last climb past Lipson Vale Junction and up past Mannamead signal box. We continued to pull into Mutley tunnel and then closing the regulator we dropped down through the redundant platforms of the closed Mutley station and then into Plymouth (North Road), here Percy applied our brake and we stopped at 5.35 am.

We both went forward to watch the assisting engine's fireman uncouple and noticed that he had considerable difficulty in doing this because they were frozen

'Grange' class 4-6-0 No. 6825 *Llanvair Grange* has just arrived with the 8.30 am Penzance to Paddington express at Plymouth (North Road) on 30th August, 1946. 'Castle' class 4-6-0 No. 5050 *Earl of St Germans* took over from here to Paddington.   *Roger Venning*

'Hall' class 4-6-0 No. 4912 *Berrington Hall* with the 5.00 pm Taunton to Exeter stopping train leaving Norton Fitzwarren with Collett Goods 0-6-0 No. 2211 on the down relief platform with the 5.00 pm Taunton to Minehead train, 27th September, 1947.   *Roger Venning*

together. When eventually the vacuum pipe coupling was prised apart we could see that the mouth of our front vacuum hose was blocked by a solid plug of ice which had formed there. This explained why the driver of the assisting engine could not control the brakes during our descents from Dainton and Hemerdon.

The assisting engine went forward to turn on the turntable that lay inside the triangle created by the junction of lines in and out of Millbay and the main line to Cornwall. This engine would be used to assist the 8.30 am service from Plymouth to Paddington.

We had to take the empty stock of our train down to Millbay and dispose of it in the carriage sidings. The fire was definitely looking the worse for wear and was not generating much heat but the pressure gauge still indicated that we had about 200 lb., hopefully enough for the shunting movements that lay ahead.

As soon as we had a signal from the shunter and the signals were clear we steamed down the incline into Millbay station. We now had to push the carriages back up into Harwell Street Sidings, the approach to which was on a gradient of about 1 in 80. By now the boiler pressure had dropped to about 180 lb. and it was going to take all the fine judgment that Percy could muster to propel our 10-coach train up into the siding at a bit of a run and then stop without knocking the stop blocks down. To add to our problems the siding only had sufficient capacity for the stock we were attempting to shunt. We began to set back at a steady rate in the hope of gaining enough momentum to allow us to get up into the siding. Percy shut off just a moment too soon and gravity prevented our first attempt at getting into this siding. He opened the regulator but the diminishing boiler pressure meant that we lacked the power to overcome the weight of the load. Seeing that it was still clear to go forward without colliding with anything he let the engine roll forward about a coach length and then lifted the regulator wide open and the train rolled back into the siding with only a slight bump against the stop blocks. The shunter was satisfied and we were able to return, tender first, to Laira Shed. It was still a freezing cold morning outside and, having no shovelling to do, I squeezed myself up between the cab sheet and the boiler on my side in an attempt to keep warm. We went to the cabin at Laira where we had a can of tea and ate breakfast. The foreman told us that he had no return working for us and so we returned to Taunton as passengers on the 8.30 am service to Paddington.

One of the regular turns covered by the Taunton No. 1 Passenger Link was the working of the down 'North Mail' from Taunton to Plymouth. Although this was not a particularly glamorous train with only moderate timings between stops its working seemed to be packed with incidents, some of which I have related in the first volume of these memoirs.

This train rolled into the down relief platform from Bristol one winter's morning at 8.07 am as usual. On relieving the Bristol crew the fireman said that there was so much leakage from the steam heating that he was shutting it off during station stops so that he could see the guard. I left it shut off and as soon as the station work was over the platform inspector came forward giving us the 'Right away'. However because the cloud of leaking steam had dispersed I could see clearly back along the whole length of the train, and I took no notice of him. He came up to the engine and asked if I was refusing to accept his signal.

'County' class 4-6-0 No. 1022 *County of Northampton* at Plymouth (North Road) station with a stopping train to Penzance in July 1947.   *Roger Venning*

No. 1024 *County of Pembroke* with the 5.00 pm Taunton to Exeter stopping train leaving Norton Fitzwarren station on 3rd October, 1947.   *Roger Venning*

I asked him where the guard was. He was furious and marched back along the platform blowing his whistle as he went. When he was about halfway along the train I saw the guard hurrying out of the refreshment rooms carrying a cup of tea. He dashed to his van, put his cup down, picked up his green flag and waved us away.

About a month later as I was signing on around midday when I was called to the office and was confronted by a footplate inspector. He told me that a platform inspector had reported me for delaying the departure of a train. I explained the circumstances and the sharp frosty conditions that prevailed at the time of the alleged incident. He took me to see the platform inspector who argued his case very strongly. The footplate inspector told me to be more tolerant in future, refusing to consider the possible consequences of leaving without our guard!

Throughout my career I have always been prepared to experiment in order to improve on existing practices. One of the observations that I made during this period was that the new tenders that came attached to the recently introduced '10XX' 'County' class 4-6-0 always appeared to be too closely coupled to the leading coach of the train. The evidence for this lay in the fact that the buffer springs were being over compressed but various enquiries assured me that they were the same standard Great Western design that we had always used. I remained unconvinced because when coupling up to a train with a standard Collett-designed 4,000 gallon tender it was standard practice to leave four threads of the screwed portion showing between the knuckles of the coupling. If this standard was applied when coupling up a '10XX' class it appeared much too short as the engine had to ram hard up against the train in order to lift the coupling over the hook of the coach. I expressed my thoughts to Fred Mogg and he agreed to have a look after I had coupled up. I cleaned and oiled our tender coupling until it worked really smoothly and Fred backed the engine up to the train so that the buffers just touched. He then blew up a vacuum so that the brakes were off on both the engine and the tender. This meant that when I had hooked the coupling over the coach I could tighten the adjusting screw as far as I was able to and see how much I had compressed the buffers. Fred came back and observed this because he wanted to assure himself that the train was securely attached to the tender. When I had coupled up the vacuum pipes it was possible to see that there were six threads showing between the knuckles of the coupling. From that time on I always made sure that there were six threads showing when coupling up a '10XX' class to a train.

Having arrived at Plymouth one day in 1947 with the down 'North Mail' we were waiting for our return working with the 11.05 am Penzance to Paddington service which was due to depart at 1.55 pm. Our locomotive this day was '10XX' class No. 1017 *County of Hereford* and it was all prepared ready for us to take off shed. But I made a point of going around the back of the tender to clean and oil the tender coupling before we left Laira to run back down to North Road. By 1.30 pm we were in position and waiting the arrival of our train and at 1.48 pm it ran in behind a '68XX' 'Grange' class 4-6-0. As soon as it had cut off and gone to shed our ground disc signal was lowered and we set back onto our eight-coach train. I got down and coupled up leaving six threads showing between the knuckles of the coupling and when I climbed up onto the platform I found myself staring into the face of running inspector Button of Newton Abbot. He had observed me coupling up and wanted to discuss what I had done. Fred now joined the inspector and myself on the platform and we explained our practice to him. He told us that there had been many complaints of rough riding and of fore and aft oscillation in trains that had been hauled by '10XX' class engines. He doubted if our small adjustment of the tension in the coupling would make any difference but he said that he would be riding in the second coach of the train to see if he would experience any irregular movement worth reporting. He instructed Fred to pay no attention to his presence in the train and to drive just as he would do normally.

Having been given the 'Right away' from the guard we pulled out of North Road with the full 280 lb. of boiler pressure showing on the gauge. After one or two revolutions of the driving wheels Fred closed the cylinder cocks and before we got to Mutley tunnel the exhaust from our chimney was lovely and clear with not a hint of damp steam showing. We drifted down the gradient past Mannamead signal box and on to Lipson Vale and Laira. I had the blower turned on slightly while we were drifting under light steam in order to keep the firebox as hot as possible but as soon as we passed through Tavistock Junction I turned it off because the exhaust sharpened on the approach to Plympton and became a beautifully crisp staccato bark as we got stuck into Hemerdon Bank. The high working pressure of these engines coupled with the original single chimney resulted in a remarkable exhaust sound. I continued to shovel coal into the white hot firebox and the effect was magic. Even with the exhaust injector full on since passing Laira the safety valves erupted after we had climbed only the first few chains of the 1 in 41 gradient and the roar of steam escaping at 280 lb. coupled with the sheer volume of the exhaust created a crescendo of noise that will never be heard again. Fred set the reversing gear in 35 per cent cut-off and with the regulator wide open we stormed up Hemerdon in fine style. Even though the safety valves closed before we reached the summit of the climb, the pressure never dropped below 270 lb. The rest of the run to Newton Abbot was uneventful and when we had stopped at the platform Mr Button came forward and complimented Fred on the run. He also said that my theory on the adjustment of the coupling screw might be the answer to the problem because he had felt no fore and aft oscillation, or any form of rough riding, during the run up from Plymouth.

We carried on to Exeter where the 5-coach Kingswear portion was added making our load up to 13. On the run to Taunton Fred favoured 22 per cent cut-off and the regulator ¾ open for miles on end. I kept the exhaust injector running the whole way to Whiteball, firing steadily to keep a relatively even fire burning brightly all over the grate. The rate of feed of the exhaust injector was set low so that although we left Exeter with the water almost out of sight in the top of the glass, by the time we reached Cullompton the water level had dropped about an inch below the top nut as the boiler was evaporating slightly more water than was being fed into it. Between Tiverton Junction and Sampford Peverell the water had come down to just over half a glass, but on the climb to Burlescombe and Whiteball it was up to ¾ full again because of the gradient. As we passed Whiteball box Fred slammed the regulator shut and then opened it again to the coasting position in order to keep the lubricator working. The exhaust injector blew out and I went over to Fred's side of the cab to set the live steam injector working, because as we accelerated down the 1 in 127 gradient the level in the water gauge had dipped to ¼ full. As we burst out of the eastern portal of Whiteball tunnel I fired another round of about 10 shovelfuls of coal around the firebox and then cracked the blower on, just about ⅛ of a turn , in order to keep a good draught running through the fire. I fired a similar round between Bradford Crossing and Victory Siding signal box. All the time the water had been climbing in the gauge and when we ran into Taunton the boiler was full and the firebox had a beautiful white hot fire, ready for my relief to have a 'royal' start on his journey to Paddington.

'51XX' class 2-6-2 tank No. 5172 was still a Taunton engine when I became a fireman. It was used on the Wellington banking turn, heavy passenger trains on the Minehead branch and even on the No. 1 Passenger Link. I vividly recall one Sunday when we used this engine to work a Taunton to Kingswear stopping train. We booked on at 9.00 am and went to the station where the engine was already attached to the train having being prepared by the shed prep. link. The 9.15 am all stations to Kingswear was a heavy train and was usually allocated a '49XX' or a '68XX' but on this occasion the turntable was out of action at Kingswear. The work was well within the capacity of the locomotive but water would be a problem, particularly if we needed to top up at Exeter because this would mean having to detach the engine from the train and going to the South Devon Sidings. Fred Mogg, my regular driver, could be relied upon to work the engine so as to be as economical with the water as possible. He used the ejector to create a vacuum for the brake but as soon as we were moving he would shut it off and let the pump do all the work. Similarly I was expected to show skill in managing the boiler by having full working pressure without letting the safety valves lift or by letting water run to waste by permitting the injectors to overflow. The danger of scalding Permanent Way workers with a jet of boiling water when operating an injector was well known and all firemen were required to exercise extreme vigilance. The technique that I used when water needed to be conserved was to turn on the steam supply to the injector first, followed by opening the water valve to a pre-marked position. This pre-marked position was a chalk mark on the water valve indicating the point where the injector 'picked up'. Similarly when shutting off the injector I shut off the water valve first and then the steam supply. This practice paid off well because when we arrived at Exeter we had only used a third of our water tank's capacity, leaving us with enough to get to Kingswear. However, when we arrived at Dawlish we were told to expect a long delay because of single line working between here and Teignmouth. Just to add to the problem the pilotman was waiting at Teignmouth for an up train and I remember saying to Fred, 'Bang goes our meal break at Kingswear!' Fortunately we had drawn up by the water column at Dawlish and so we took water here while we waited.

One hour later, with the pilotman on board, we departed for Teignmouth eventually arriving at Kingswear at about 1.15 pm. Here we detached and ran around our train and left, bunker first, at 1.30 pm. We were 'right time' again

'King' class 4-6-0 No. 6021 *King Richard II* with the 8.00 am Penzance to Paddington express near Bishopsteignton on 21st September, 1948.   *Pursey Short*

and there would be no need to take water when we arrived at Newton Abbot where we had 15 minutes to wait. While we were drinking a lid of tea and eating our sandwiches at Newton Abbot an anxious platform inspector came up and asked us if we wanted to go to the shed and turn but we told him we were happy as we were. There was a Newton Abbot '51XX' tank, facing the right way, in the loco spur and no doubt had we said we needed to turn we would have been told to change footplates and take on this unknown quantity. We continued bunker first to Exeter where we left our passenger coaches. After taking water we departed with two milk tanks for Tiverton Junction where we picked up a further three. With this light load we ran to Wellington where we had to shunt into the milk loading siding, picking up five loaded milk tanks, two of which were road tanks mounted on special rail wagons. It was now 6.00 pm and our shift would end when we arrived back at Taunton. No. 5172 would then be required to work the 7.20 pm stopping train to Exeter and so I set about building a suitable fire to hand over to the fireman on this duty. We left Wellington at 6.30 pm and ran to Taunton, where I was surprised to see a another engine standing at the head of the 7.20 pm stopping train. We took our engine to shed where I reported to the foreman that I had left a high fire in the engine because I had not been notified of any alterations to the booked working.

After I was made a driver at Taunton I drove No. 5172 many times, mostly on the banking turn at Wellington or on passenger trains on the Minehead line. On one occasion with this engine we left Minehead with the 2.20 pm express service for Paddington which we took as far as Taunton. The load was nine coaches equal to 285 tons and as usual No. 5172 rose to the challenge and performed magnificently. I greatly regret that No. 5172 didn't survive to be preserved because it was such a regular good performer! It remained at Taunton until its withdrawal in 1958.

Chapter Eight

Some Driving Turns

On being promoted to driver I now had to assume the responsibilities for the proper preparation of any engine before we left shed, even for the humble shunting turns which I worked frequently at this stage of my career.

Having signed on duty, I would first study the notice board for any late notices that had not appeared in the weekly notices. Next I would locate the engine booked for the duty where I would hope to meet my fireman, who should have unlocked the toolbox and put out the oil cans in which the driver would collect the allowance of oil for this turn from the stores. Before going to the stores I would test the water gauge, satisfy myself that the fusible plugs and tubes were in good condition and that the fireman was attending to his duties properly.

In the case of a shunting engine you would be allowed four pints of oil for any 24 hour period. The allowance would consist of three pints of engine oil for use in axle boxes and bearings, and one pint of cylinder oil. In addition to the lubricating oil one pint of paraffin would be issued for use in the flare lamp and gauge glass lamp.

On returning to the engine from the stores the driver's duties were chiefly concerned with the lubrication. The three pints of lubricating oil had to be carefully rationed around the engine. It was important for me to work to a system and before going underneath to lubricate the engine I would make sure that the handbrake was applied firmly, the reversing lever was in mid-gear and that a 'Not to be Moved' board was exhibited on the buffer beam. Going underneath I would oil the four eccentrics, all the valve gear motion pins, the big end and small end bearings, the slipper blocks of the cross heads, the oil cups on the slide bars, the piston and valve spindle gland oil cups and finally the lubricator on the vacuum pump.

Corks played an important part in the lubrication of the valve gear, connecting and coupling rods. Corks were used to seal the oil reservoirs of many of the principal bearings in the locomotive and it was important for me to check that not only was the cork in good condition, but also that it was the correct cork and that it had been inserted in the prescribed manner. While some corks were plain, being similar to the sort that would have been used as a stopper for a medicine bottle of that period, some corks had a cane inserted through the middle of them. These 'cane' corks permitted more air to enter the reservoir of a big end bearing which, by preventing a vacuum forming in that chamber, ensured a continuous flow of oil to the moving surfaces. After a bearing had been re-metalled and it was still a tight fit a driver would be given the job of fitting new corks to all oil reservoirs of the valve gear, connecting and coupling rods. A driver would always have a few new corks in his overall pockets when preparing engines in case he found some which, through repeated use, were going further down into the threaded filler hole of the reservoir. In such cases it was possible for the cork eventually to cap the top of the tube and effectively cut off the oil supply and lead to seizure. If you had

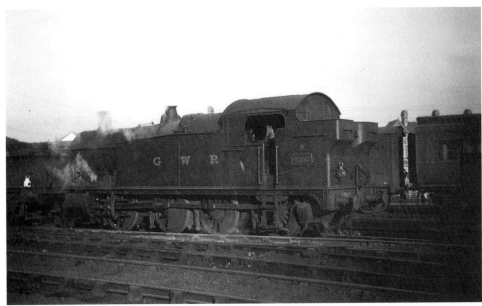

Newport Ebbw Junction-allocated '42XX' class 2-8-0T No. 4260 is a visitor at Taunton Shed on 17th December, 1946.   *Roger Venning*

'Dukedog' class 4-4-0 No. 9010 awaits the signal to proceed from Taunton Shed to East Yard where it will collect the branch goods train to Watchet and Minehead, January 1947.
                                                                                Roger Venning

Fireman Bob Chudleigh is seen on the footplate of 0-6-0PT No. 6407 which is the West End station pilot on a cold winter's day in January 1947. Fairwater bridge forms the backdrop for this view.   *Roger Venning*

Driver Ron Eldrick and fireman Stone pose for the photographer next to their engine, 0-6-0PT No. 4663, at Dulverton in 1950. The engine had worked the 8.20 am goods from Taunton.
Tony Harvey/Roger Venning Collection

been fortunate to have been the regular driver of the same engine for a week or so you might notice that one or more of the bearings was using too much oil, in which case you would replace a cane cork with a plain one to restrict the oil flow to an acceptable rate.

While oiling the slidebars and piston rod gland oil cups I would lift out the 'tail trimmings' to make sure that they were in good order. If they had started to disintegrate, become dirty or were missing I would have to fit new trimmings made from five strands of worsted wool secured to a short length of twisted iron wire. It was amazing just how much oil the wicking action of this trimming would carry to the piston rod or slide bars. Tail trimmings were only used on sliding surfaces. On rotating surfaces, such as big ends, a 'plug trimming' was used to restrict the flow of lubricant to bearing surfaces from the oil reservoir. The 'plug trimming' was made of seven strands of worsted wool and was inserted far enough into the feeder tube to ensure a small accumulation of oil above the trimming, but not so far into the tube that it touched the bearing surface. Without a trimming fitted the contents of a big end bearing oil reservoir would soon empty. In later years the plug trimmings in big end bearings were replaced by a metal triangular-sectioned restrictor plug.

As I went around to the front of the engine I would make sure that the fireman had tightened the smokebox door firmly and that the front footplate was clear of any ash or spilled sand. Returning to the footplate I would then cheek that the vacuum brake, injectors and the sanding gear were all working. Only then would I be satisfied that the engine was ready for work.

I consider myself fortunate as I was never involved in a derailment or a serious collision during the whole of my footplate career. However one small incident did occur shortly after I had been promoted to driver when shunting on the night turn in the West Yard opposite Taunton School. Our shunting movements took us back and forward under Staplegrove bridge which carried the main road

Taunton West Station signal box.   *Exe Rail*

from Taunton to Barnstaple and Minehead and we tended to shunt by habit. On hearing the signal whistles from the shunter the regulator was opened, four exhaust beats from the engine, shut the regulator and apply the brake, wait for the cloud of steam to clear so that you can see the shunter again. On this particular night we were waiting under Staplegrove bridge when we saw the head shunter walking towards us displaying a red aspect from his hand lamp, when he got up to the engine he told me that he had a wagon derailed. I put the brake on hard and told the fireman that I was going to have a look at what had happened. There were nine wagons attached to the engine and when I got to the first set of handpoints there was a van with two of its wheels down between the rails. Apparently the point operating mechanism had been starved of lubrication and had become stiff. Having knocked off one wagon from the raft the undershunter had tried to turn the points for the next shunt. The point had proved too stiff for him to operate and the wheels of the on-coming wagon had split the points and become derailed. When my fireman joined us I suggested that we get the re-railing ramps out of the tool box on the shunters truck attached to the engine. These funnel shaped ramps pressed from ½ in. thick steel plate were designed to be placed over the rail ahead of the wheels that had been derailed. The wagon would then be drawn slowly over the ramps which would re-align the wheels over rails and 'Hey-Presto!' the wagon should be back on the rails. We followed this drill on this occasion and, when the van had been re-railed, Dennis, the undershunter, came out with a prize comment when he said, 'I always wondered what those things were for!' We carried on shunting and then about half an hour after the incident the night turn yard inspector, Bert Frost, arrived on foot from the East Yard. He came alongside the cab and said, 'Some bloody fool rung me up to say that you were off the road down here and blocking the yard!' At first I denied all knowledge of any incident but the head shunter told him what had happened and indicated to him which wagon had been derailed. Bert Frost then sent for the train examiner to come and put the gauge over the wheels to ensure that they had not been displaced. Evidently it was the signalman in the West Junction signal box who had phoned him.

On a Sunday morning in the Spring of 1950 I was booked out on a permanent way train in the Chard branch. The worksheet said 'Unloading rails' and we were due on duty at 5.15 am and off shed at 6.00 am. The engine we had was '2251' class 0-6-0 No. 2230, which was fitted with a vacuum braked tender. We prepared the engine and took it across to the Engineer's yard situated opposite Taunton East Junction signal box where we met the guard and buffered up to our train. We had two wagons of ballast and three 'Ganes' (long bogie wagons with side bolsters), loaded with rails. I told my fireman that even though it was only five wagons they amounted to a pretty heavy load and that I would want plenty of steam to get this train to Chard. When all was ready we advised the signalman, the ground disc was cleared and we pulled steadily out of the Engineer's Sidings and onto the up relief. I could tell by the regulator opening that we had a heavy load behind us but we steamed steadily to Creech Junction, where unfortunately we were stopped by signals. The signalman had stopped us to ensure that we were the right train because another PW train was due to go to Somerton that morning. He handed us the Creech Junction-Ilminster

Mogul No. 7304 departs Barnstaple Junction with a train for Taunton. An ex-SR Bulleid Pacific can be seen on shed in the background.   *Exe Rail*

BR Standard 2-6-2T No. 82030 waits to leave Thornfalcon, on the Chard branch, with a train for Taunton.   *Exe Rail*

token (Hatch Beauchamp box was still open at this time but switched out) and we then faced the 1 in 100 climb from a dead stand up to the bridge that carried the branch over the River Tone. The fireman had a good fire in the box and pressure was nearly on the red line of the gauge. We needed it because the '2251s' were only classed as 'B' group engines on the power classification scale and we really needed something stronger this morning!

We pulled away from Creech Junction with the reverser in full forward gear and the regulator half open but it was not long before the driving wheels began to lose their grip on the rails. I was ready for this and slammed the regulator shut before opening it again to the quarter-open position, then I opened the sand valve in an attempt to regain adhesion. Finding that the wheels now gripped the rails I opened the regulator wide and we stormed up the incline to the bridge. The gradients eased and then dropped a little along the embankment towards Thornfalcon and the sand valve was closed. Nevertheless the regulator was still wide open and the cut-off set at 40 per cent as the climb began again before we reached the station and steepened to 1 in 80 as we passed under the bridge which carried the A358 over the railway. This climb continued for a mile up past Ash, where the line reached its summit in a deep cutting crossed by three bridges. Here I closed the regulator to the drifting position and we rolled down past Bath House Farm at 1 in 80 for half a mile before a short level section where I opened the regulator again. The climb resumed at 1 in 80 and we crossed the A358 and then ran parallel with the road for a quarter of a mile or so before we curved left into a deep cutting and the depths of Hatch tunnel. This tunnel was only 152 yds long and constructed to take a double track but once we are out the other side and through the station we were on the largely level block section with only gentle grades between here and Ilminster. Nevertheless the crossing keeper had heard us coming at Spekes Wood and we opened up a bit on the climb into Ilminster where the permanent way gang had assembled. A bit of planning now took place between the ourselves on the footplate, the guard and the ganger as to what we were going to do. While his gang piled into the brake van the ganger came up and informed us that he wanted the rails off-loaded near Sunshine Cider Mill, about a mile on the Donyatt side of Chard Central. The rails would be pulled off the wagon using a wire rope which he would fix to the track. I replied that it was going to be difficult because there was another 1 in 80 gradient at that point and in any case the roller was on the Chard end of the 'Gane', so it would be best to go on to Chard Central, run around the train and then return to the point where the rails were to be off-loaded.

With everybody on board we set off from Ilminster up the gentle grade to Donyatt Halt and on to Chard. The final three miles into Chard Central was quite a climb with gradients as steep as 1 in 76. As we ran past Sunshine Cider Mill we could see the derelict remains of the incline where the tub boats on the old Chard Canal had reached the final summit pound of this erstwhile inland waterway. We pulled into Chard Central, ran around the train and put the brake van into a siding. We then coupled up to the Taunton end of the train, pulled back and only with a considerable effort managed to push the train back into the yard. Here we detached the two ballast wagons because they were not being discharged until later in the week. We then pulled out of this siding and pushed our three 'Ganes' back onto our brake van.

0-6-0PT No. 3736 and 'B Set' Nos. 6359/6361 wait to depart Chard Junction with the 7.26 pm to Taunton on 7th July, 1962.   *H.C. Casserley*

The station at Chard Central is starting to lose its battle with nature. BR Standard 2-6-4T No. 82030 waits to depart for Chard Junction with the 8.43 pm on 7th July, 1962.   *H.C. Casserley*

The ganger then explained exactly where he wanted me to stop for him to off-load the rails so I opened the ejector to have the additional braking power of the tender. As soon as my fireman released the handbrake we started to roll down the grade. Travelling at a very modest rate we were approaching the spot where we had to stop, I got the fireman to apply the tender brake firmly and I was already applying the brake to control our speed. Suddenly there was a lot of shouting from the brakevan and the ganger signalled me to stop. I made a full application of the vacuum and steam brake but this was of no avail because we rolled past the spot the ganger wanted by about a train's length before we actually stopped.

The ganger came back and asked me to push the train back, but my fireman, anticipating that we would not be needing a full head of steam at this stage, had let the pressure fall back to about 160 lb. Try as I might the engine could not push the train back up the grade. I then suggested that we could off-load some rails here and then complete the job on the section we had run past when the load had decreased. By the time we had completed unloading the engine had a full head of steam and it was now easy enough for the engine to propel the near empty wagons back up the gradient.

Later day in th e day when I was disposing of the engine at Taunton I found out that the vacuum brake cylinder on the tender was as good as useless as it came off as soon as it had been applied. This indicated that the rubber sealing ring around the vacuum brake piston head was permitting air to pass and not holding the brake on. I left a report of this fault with the shed foreman.

Taunton always seemed to be a popular place for engines to fail for one reason or another. I have known of cases where engines that could be considered to have 'failed' close to a larger shed being sent on to Taunton so that it could officially fail there. An incidence of this practice occurred when I relieved a Nottingham to Paignton train at Bristol (Temple Meads) when I was still a fireman. The driver we were relieving said that he had wired ahead for a fresh engine because a big end was knocking, but all that Bath Road did was to send a fitter to the station to examine the reported fault. He duly removed the cap nut from the crank pin, eased the big end journal forward and doused the crank pin in thick cylinder oil and assured my driver that it would make Taunton. He said that he would phone ahead for a fresh engine but, as expected, Taunton had no suitable replacement engine and so it proceeded on to Exeter doing more damage as each mile went by!

Taunton would do its best to find a replacement engine but as Clive Bousfield's photograph (*next page*) shows what it managed to find wasn't always appropriate. This photograph shows what happened when a 'King' failed with down 'Limited' in September 1947 and here can be seen pulling away from Taunton behind a WD 'Austerity' 2-8-0.

At every stage of my railway career I always prided myself on being resourceful and capable of showing initiative when it was required. An Autumn evening in September 1950 found me and my fireman on a shed relief duty. Around about 8.30 pm the foreman gave us 'Castle' class 4-6-0 No. 5003 *Lulworth Castle* to prepare as up line spare engine so as to be ready to cover any contingency that might occur between then and when it was required for the 6.35 am passenger service to Bristol the following morning. We had plenty of time for

A 'WD' 2-8-0 leaves Taunton's platform 5 with the down 'Cornish Riviera Express', after the failure of the original train engine (a 'King' class locomotive). The photograph was taken from the tender of 'Bulldog' class No. 3361, September 1947.

Clive Bousfield/Roger Venning Collection

this preparation and having drawn the oil allowance from the stores I attended to every lubrication point while my fireman endeavoured to maintain a black fire so that the safety valves wouldn't be blowing all night. This proved to be more of a problem for him than he had imagined because there was already rather more fire in the box than was necessary and even when he had added all the fuel spilled on the footplate during coaling he could see that it was still going to be difficult to keep it quiet. At about 11.30 pm we had just finished filling the tender from the water crane and my fireman had just closed the lid when we heard an up train running into the station; as it passed the back of Taunton West Station signal box the metallic clank of a failed big end bearing echoed around the neighbourhood. Obviously our engine was going to be needed and so I told my fireman who had been trying to keep the engine quiet to open the back dampers and put the blower on to bring the fire back to life. The train was the 7.00 pm Penzance to Paddington TPO and I knew that it was important to prevent any delay to this service, so I blew the brakes off and reversed the engine up to the exit where I blew one long whistle and one short one, being the code to the signalman for us to come off shed. The signalman came to the window and I shouted that I was the fresh engine for the up 'Postal', he then set the points and we ran out onto the down relief, crossed over to the down main and ran through the station to stop alongside the engine with the big end failure.

I shouted across to the driver asking him if he wanted a fresh engine? 'How the hell did you know?', asked the driver and I told him that I had heard the problem as they were running in. We exchanged footplates and I phoned Taunton East Junction signal box and told them I was taking the failed engine to shed and that the engine standing on the up main was to work the train forward. With the road set we clanked our way back to shed with 'Castle' class 4-6-0 No. 5071 *Spitfire*.

'Castle' class 4-6-0 No. 5033 *Broughton Castle* hauls a Manchester-Plymouth express through Dunball on 20th September, 1947. The Dunball Wharf branch can be seen crossing the main line in the foreground. *Pursey Short*

When we were back within shed limits I examined the engine all round before going onto the firepit. I found the right-hand inside big end to be the culprit because it was mighty hot. We locked up the tools and were walking back to the stores when Fred Green, the night foreman, approached in a very excited condition demanding to know where we had been and where was No. 5003.

'Well', I said, '5003 is on its way to London'.

'What!', said Fred 'The up 'Postal' wants a fresh engine up at the station'.

'No it doesn't', I replied, 'It should be running through Bridgwater about now with 5003 on the front.

At first Fred couldn't believe his ears but when he calmed down I told him all about it and he was so pleased he let us go home about 1½ hours early. That was after I had completed a repair ticket for No. 5071.

Around about the time of the Coronation of Queen Elizabeth II the turntable at Taunton was out of commission for heavy maintenance and no engine could be turned. This created all sorts of problems, particularly for Mr Aston, the shedmaster, who adhered to a very strict rota for boiler washing. It was arranged that all engines that needed their boilers washing out were to be stabled just inside the shed doorways on the incoming and outgoing roads. Various drivers were given the job of oiling underneath all engines as they stood over the inspection pit when they were taking coal. They were then shunted into the adjacent carriage sidings in the order of their allocated duties where their preparation would be completed by the crews after they had signed on. The disruption caused few problems for the tank engines used on the Minehead, Yeovil and Chard branches, and during this time the Barnstaple branch was worked by '2251' 0-6-0 tender engines which could be turned on the small turntable at Durston.

The larger engines created more of an operational headache and special working diagrams were drawn up. These ensured that engines working west to Exeter and Newton Abbot were next day booked on a Bristol turn so that they would return to the shed facing the fight way for the following day. One of

Collett Goods 0-6-0 No. 2215 is seen at Norton Fitzwarren with the 5.00 pm Taunton-Minehead train on 13th September, 1947. The indicator below the signal shows 'M'Head', for the Minehead line.   *Roger Venning*

'51XX' class 2-6-2T No. 5172 departs Norton Fitzwarren with the 9.40 am Paddington to Minehead (Saturdays-only) train on 13th September, 1947. The 'M' disc denotes a Minehead branch train.   *Roger Venning*

'57XX' class 0-6-0PT is ready and waiting to depart from Minehead with the 10.50 am to Taunton on 15th July, 1958.   *R.M. Casserley*

Priaire tank No. 4103 awaits its passengers in this 1960s view of Minehead station.   *Exe Rail*

these special diagrams involving the working of a '63XX' on the 8.05 am Taunton to Barnstaple. When it returned with the 1.11 pm from Barnstaple it was diagramed to be relieved and work the 4.35 pm passenger to Bristol returning with the 8.40 pm service to Taunton.

I found myself booked to work the 4.35 pm to Bristol and back with my regular fireman, who at that time was Michael Nott. We signed on at 3.20 pm and walked to the station to relieve the crew of the 1.11 pm from Barnstaple. The west end carriage shunter came to the back of the train and took the coaches away and we went forward. After taking water from the column we then backed onto a train of six coaches which was standing in No. 9 bay platform. The previous fireman had kept a good high fire in the firebox and all that Michael had to do was shovel the coal forward on the tender. I went around with the oil can topping up the various oiling points where necessary. The engine was No. 6372 which was always a good performer on the undulating Barnstaple branch and today would provide an opportunity to see how she would perform on the main line. The guard gave us all the train load information and I tested the vacuum brake. At 4.35 pm the signal was lowered, the guard waved his green flag and we were away. With the reversing lever in full forward gear, the cylinder cocks open just in case any condensate had accumulated in the cylinders, I eased the regulator open. After two turns of the wheels I could see the cylinders were quite dry so I closed the cocks and pulled the lever back to 45 per cent. Once we were past East Junction box the signals gave us a completely clear road ahead, so I shortened the cut-off further to 30 per cent and lifted the regulator until it was ¾ open. Now a mile out of Taunton and running towards Bathpool bridge I checked the hydrostatic lubricator and adjusted it to pass five drops of oil a minute. This service stopped at all the stations to Weston-super-Mare, the timings were undemanding and we had no trouble in making a right time arrival there.

From here we were to run fast to Bristol (Temple Meads), stopping only at Yatton. The train then formed part of an express service to Paddington with the usual 'Castle' at its head. While we were standing at the platform, Michael went to the front of the engine and altered the headcode to 'A' class placing a lamp on the brackets over each buffer. I had 12 years experience as a fireman working with a quite a large number of drivers and I always took a close interest in how they drove this class of engine. As a result I had developed my own ideas as to how to get the best out of them and this fast run to Bristol would provide an opportunity to put it to the test.

As soon as Michael called out 'Right away!' I re-checked that the signals were clear ahead at Weston-super-Mare, East box, and opened the regulator to the halfway position. As we accelerated briskly away I shortened the cut-off to 35 per cent and lifted the regulator wide open. After half a mile or so I brought the reversing lever back to 25 per cent cut-off and we shot through Weston Milton Halt. I had to shut off here for the 40 mph speed limit at Worle Junction. The engine was performing so well that I had to let the vacuum drop to 15 inches in applying the brake and then had to use the ejector to blow the brakes off. We rolled smoothly over the junction pointwork and then I lifted the regulator fully open and put the reversing lever in the last notch before mid-gear at 22 per cent cut-off.

Mike had maintained a good head of steam and had built a lovely 'haycock' fire. With her safety valves simmering the old girl sensed a freedom that was not found on the steep gradients and sinuous curves of the Barnstaple branch and, like a horse let loose from a paddock, she started to gallop. The excess pressure valves popped away until she really got into her stride but we roared over the level crossing at Puxton & Worle and we were really motoring along the long straight towards Yatton. As we sped over the next level crossing at Huish, we got the ATC bell for Yatton West and I closed the regulator to the position where the jockey valve still maintained lubrication and put the reverser in the drifting notch at 45 per cent cut-off. Applying the brakevalve we came gently to a stop at Yatton station with the engine just the Bristol side of the footbridge. On receiving the 'right away' I opened the regulator no more than ¾ wide to avoid any slipping and once on the move brought the reversing lever back to 35 per cent cut-off. After passing Yatton East box. I could see all the signals were clear for Claverham, I brought the lever back to 22 per cent cut-off and opened the regulator wide. I wanted to enjoy the rest of this flying run to Bristol. From Yatton the line climbs gently for seven miles to Flax Bourton on gradients averaging about 1 in 250. Our engine appeared not to notice their existence and soon Nailsea & Backwell flashed by and the ATC bell rang out for Flax Bourton. I asked Mike to stop firing here and let the boiler come down to enable us to keep the engine quiet while we were in Bristol. We sped through Flax Bourton station, into the short tunnel and out into the long cutting that leads all the way to Long Ashton platform. The bell rang out for the IBS signals between Flax Bourton and South Liberty. I shut down the regulator to ¼ open and allowed No. 6372 her last bit of speed before passing through West Depot Yard, Parson Street, Malago Vale and Bedminster. Here a firm brake application had to be made to enable us to make a comfortable stop, dead on time, in No. 6 platform at Bristol (Temple Meads).

Mike got down and uncoupled the engine and we pulled forward to Bristol East box where the electric ground indicator signal behind our tender lit up to say 'Engine Line No. 1'. We reversed back into Bath Road Shed and joined a long queue of engines on the coal road. We planned to fill the tender to capacity here; our shed master would appreciate it if we could avoid all unneccessary movements back at Taunton while the turntable was out of use. We managed to get 10 tubs of coal loaded onto the tender and with our firebox still full Mike only needed to fire as far as Weston-super-Mare on the return journey and hence made little in-road into our fuel supply. The 8.40 pm service stopped at all stations and provided little opportunity for the spirited running we had enjoyed earlier in the day. We took water from Creech troughs before we arrived at Taunton and when we had disposed of our train we took No. 6372 to shed, leaving her on the fire pit. As soon as the fire, ashpan and smokebox had been cleaned it would be stabled in the siding ready to work the 8.05 am to Barnstaple the next day.

Because of the war and the period of austerity that followed we had to wait until 1953 for our first family holiday at the seaside. Hayle in Cornwall was our chosen destination but the English climate found us making an early return home on the Friday morning of our week away. The best service was the 12.00 midday service from Penzance to Manchester which left Hayle at 12.21 pm and then called at most stations to Plymouth (North Road), where it arrived at 3.30 pm. We travelled in the

'King' class 4-6-0 No. 6002 *King William IV* has just relieved 'Hall' class No. 4951 *Pendeford Hall* on the up 'Cornish Riviera' at Plymouth (North Road) on 4th September, 1946. The locomotive awaits its other headlamp!   *Roger Venning*

GWR Mogul No. 6386 waits for signals to allow it to cross to the goods loop lines at Fairwater, Taunton, with an up class 'J' goods in early January 1947.   *Roger Venning*

second coach of the train and when we arrived at Plymouth I took my 12-year-old son out onto the platform to see the engines change; a 'King' class 4-6-0 backed down onto our train. The coach between us and the engine was the Travelling Post Office (TPO) which attracted the interest of my son. I asked a postal worker if the exchange apparatus was in use and he confirmed that it would be used at several points along the line that afternoon. As we progressed over the South Devon banks and on to Newton Abbot and Exeter I was able to point out various landmarks and railway installations that were familiar to me from my footplate work. As we began to accelerate up the Culm Valley I told my son to put his swimming goggles on to protect his eyes and then held onto him while he leaned out the window to watch the mail bags being exchanged as we sped towards Cullompton. Witnessing this whole operation was an experience he still remembers to this day.

By now I was working in a link which regularly covered the banking engines from Wellington to Whiteball. This particular turn meant signing on at 4.25 pm and boarding a prepared engine, usually a '51XX' tank, which was due off shed at 4.40 pm. From Taunton we were light engine to Wellington where we would be ready to bank any train that needed assistance up the last three miles to Whiteball summit.

On another 10.30 pm Wellington banking turn, this time with Norman Carpenter as my fireman, we had pushed five or six trains up to Whiteball and, with the time now approaching 5.45 am, we were expecting to be sent to shed as soon as the engine from the 5.30 am Taunton to Wellington goods was available to take over banking in between shunting duties. We were waiting in the down refuge sidings at the east end of the station and we knew that the signalman would soon want us to move to make room for the arrival of the goods train. Not wishing to disturb the sleep of the people who lived in houses close to the railway line we had let the fire die down to avoid any noise from the safety valves. The peace and quiet was suddenly disturbed by the rustling of signal wires and then the thump of the down main signal being lowered. Dismissing this as being for the anticipated goods train, I took no great notice until with a sudden woosh one of the new 'Britannia' class Pacifics passed by on the adjacent track. If any driver needed assistance from a banking engine they would give a short blast on their whistle but this morning there was not a murmur. The train was the 11.50 pm Paddington to Penzance, the down 'Owl' running about an hour late, and when it had passed us I saw our signal being lowered for us to leave the refuge siding and I was now certain that the time had come for us to make way for the freight train from Taunton. Norman unwound the handbrake and without opening the ejector or cylinder cocks I eased the regulator open and quietly passed out onto the main line and down through the station where I noticed that the down starting signal was off and assumed that the signalman wanted us safely out of the way in the bay platform at the west end of the station. I looked over to the signal box for some guidance, but the early turn signalman was just taking over from his colleague on night shift and they were engaged in a conversation. Suddenly Norman shouted 'Whoa!' I reached up and whacked the vacuum brake handle on full. Fortunately for me the crosshead pump had created a maximum vacuum and the engine stopped dead within one revolution of the wheels. Norman said, 'There's a train in front of us' and sure enough not 10 feet away was the rear coach of the 'Owl' which had stopped for assistance.

'47XX' class 2-8-0 No. 4701 at Plymouth Laira Shed on 4th September, 1946. To the right is 'Bulldog' class 4-4-0 No. 3407 *Madras* and behind it Stanier '8F' class 2-8-0 No. 8434.

Roger Venning

Now it was 'Panic Stations' because we only had 160 lb. of steam and half a glass of water. Norman turned the blower on hard, opened both dampers and fetching down the 'pricker' began to stir what fire was left in the box. Clearly we had not anticipated another trip up to Whiteball this morning but now the fire was roaring and the pressure gauge began to creep upwards. I eased forward and buffered up to the rear of the train. I blew two 'crows' on the whistle and on hearing a response from the train engine I blew the brake off, opened the regulator and began pushing! Norman had his fire well in hand now, the injector was on and feeding water into the boiler. I shouted to him, 'Not too much as we're going to shed after this trip'. Clearly he understood as he fired just enough coal for our immediate needs. We roared into Whiteball tunnel and within three minutes we were out the other side, regulator shut and brakes on to bring us to a stand by the signal box. The signalman came to the window for a quick word as he wouldn't be seeing anyone for a few hours now. He told, us we were 'Right away for shed'; we glided over the crossover and onto the up main line where I shortened the cut-off to 40 per cent reverse gear and now with the regulator just open we accelerated into the tunnel. That last trip had caught us by surprise but I had been very impressed by way my fireman had been able to rally the engine around to full working pressure in less than 10 minutes.

The night shift was always the busiest for the crews of the Wellington bankers, the highlight of the night being the banking of the down 'Tip'. This was the 10.30 pm Paddington to Plymouth express freight, which at this time was invariably headed by a '47XX' class 2-8-0 with a train of 65 standard wagons in tow. This train was booked in the down platform line at Wellington in order that the 9.50 pm. Paddington to Penzance express passenger train (via Bristol) and the Paddington to Penzance Newspaper train (via the Berks & Hants) overtake. The problem at Wellington was that the down platform road could only accommodate 60 wagons and so a particular procedure had to be followed. The banking engine selected for the down 'Tip' would stand in the goods shed on a road connected to the down platform line at the Taunton end of Wellington. The down 'Tip' would run into the platform road and would have the calling-on subsidiary signal under the down platform line starter, at the end of the platform loop, lowered. It would draw ahead far enough for the brake van to get into the loop. The signals would then be replaced to the stop position and the ground disc would be lowered at the trailing point on the down main to tell the driver to set back. The points at the Taunton end of the down platform would have been set to normal and so the train would set back into the goods shed until the brake van came to rest against the front buffer beam of the banking engine. The guard of the train would give you a note detailing the train engine's number, the number of wagons and the weight of the train. A clatter of signals would follow as all the down main line signals now showed green. After a lull of about five minutes the 9.50 pm ex-Paddington would rush through the station. After about another 10 minutes a further clattering of signals occurred indicating the road being set for the down Newspaper train which passed through the station at the same speed as the preceding express passenger train.

In a matter of minutes this train would clear the IBS (Intermediate Block Section) at Beam Bridge and we would look across to the box and see the signalman setting the road and pulling off the boards for our train. He then showed us a green light and after an exchange of two 'crows' on the whistle from both engines we began to start pushing. Knowing that the train engine and its crew had already come a long way and had further still to go before they were relieved I would usually open the regulator wide and leave the reverser set at about 40 per cent cut-off. This would ensure that this train was really hammered up the hill and any further adjustment of the cut-off position would depend upon the speed you managed to sustain. Heavy coal trains demanded a longer cut-off all the way until we entered the tunnel. Here I got into the habit of counting the rail joints through the tunnel and depending on the nature of the train if it had a vacuum head, its weight and the speed we had attained, I would ease the power down after counting 30 rail joints, there being a total of 64 through the tunnel. This was to allow the driver of the train engine to take over control of the train and decide at what speed he wished the train to descend through Burlescombe and Sampford Peverell.

When I had been a fireman on this job back in 1938/39, I was always intrigued to see the home signal of the IBS go to danger six wagon lengths before we passed it. This was because the train engine would energise the next track section 60 wagon lengths after passing the IBS stop signal.

While on the subject of signals there was an anomaly in the interlocking arrangements at Wellington signal box that remained until it was replaced by the MAS system in 1986. A signalman who had been at Wellington when the box had been replaced in the 1930s told me that he had been on duty when the Ministry of Transport inspectors came to test the new equipment. They spent a considerable amount of time working their way from one end of the box to another trying every combination of levers in an attempt to find a possible fault in the interlocking and block system. He watched all of this and noticed that they had not included one lever at the western end of the frame in their tests. This was the up advanced starter which should have been locked by the block telegraph and he demonstrated this by walking to the lever and pulling it off without getting 'Line Clear' on the block. To the best of my knowledge this fault was never rectified during the working life of Wellington signal box.

Although most of the banking work was done at night, Summer Saturdays were very hectic with a large number of down passenger trains needing assistance up the bank. Many of these would run into Wellington station with the blower hard on, obviously doing badly for steam and needing maximum assistance up the bank. The regulator would be open for the whole way through the tunnel but would be slammed shut on emerging into the daylight and then the vacuum brake firmly applied to stop by the box. As I sit here writing this I can relive all these moments again in my mind and can recall the pounding of the footplate beneath my feet.

Having banked a passenger train to Whiteball you could find that the up line would be so heavily occupied with trains that the signalman would have to give you precedence over an up express to get you back to Wellington to assist a waiting heavy down train. In these circumstances the crossover from down to up lines was quickly accomplished and a rapid descent of the bank would be made with speeds that might frequently touch the high 80s. Officially we were allowed seven minutes for a '51XX' 2-6-2 tank and eight minutes with a tender engine to return to Wellington. We would fly through the tunnel and probably pass another down train being assisted by the other banking engine around about Beam Bridge. I would have to open the blower a quarter of a turn to keep the flames in the firebox when I closed the regulator before I braked for the station, where we would cross straight over from up main to down main, stop and reverse the engine and then buffer up to the next waiting train. I would whistle two 'crows' and off up the bank again with a bright fire capable of generating all the steam we needed as we pushed as hard as we could from the rear. Up trains were streaming down the bank thick and fast and so it was possible that when we arrived at Whiteball the other banking engine would still be there. If so, we would be coupled together for the descent of the bank. Here we would both take water before uncoupling, one of us going to wait in the goods yard while the other would go to the down refuge siding. So rapid was the process of banking passenger trains on Summer Saturdays that we would sometimes do three trips up the bank before replenishing the water tanks.

This sort of work was totally different to banking freight trains when we would be pounding slowly with the reverser set at 45 per cent cut off and evaporating about 500 gallons during one ascent of the bank. At about 3.00 one morning we had just passed Beam Bridge at about 10 mph while assisting a heavy freight train when I heard my fireman shout. I looked to see the guard of the train we were banking standing in the doorway of our engine. He had crossed over to the engine from the buffers of his van and had clambered along the side of the footplate and tapped my fireman on the shoulder and frightened the living daylights out of him in the process. He then calmly asked him for a light for his cigarette before returning to his van the same way as he had come.

0-4-0ST No. 1338 was originally built for the Cardiff Railway by Messrs Kitson and Co. in 1898. She migrated to Taunton during the war years and spent most of her time shunting the labyrinth of sidings that surrounded Bridgwater Docks. Most Saturday afternoons she returned light engine to Taunton Shed to have her

Ex-Cardiff Railway 0-4-0ST No. 1338 stands in the coaling queue at Taunton on 27th September, 1947.   *Roger Venning*

Ex-Burry Port & Gwendreath Valley Railway 0-6-0ST No. 2194 *Kidwelly* is light engine on its way back to Taunton Shed after working at Dunball Docks, north of Bridgwater. It is seen here 100 yards west of Creech St Michael water troughs on 12th May, 1945. War in Europe had ceased just four days earlier.   *Pursey Short*

boiler washed out over the weekend. This engine was fitted with J. Hawthorn-Kitson's valve gear which was similar to Walschaert's gear in that the lap and lead movement was derived from the crosshead but the travel movement came from the coupling rod which drove a near vertical eccentric rod. This was in turn connected to the expansion link which it caused to oscillate about the trunnion bearings. The design had been developed for steam tramway engines where it was deemed to have an advantage in that it kept most of the valve gear linkage clear of possible roadside obstacles and obstructions.

As this engine was running along the main line back to Taunton this strange valve gear appeared to bob up and down giving the appearance of an overgrown grasshopper. Its small coal bunkers were situated either side of the firebox and in the rear sheet of the cab there was a metal door. As we passed Fordgate on one of these Saturday afternoon trips my fireman opened this door and put his shovel out the back which he then waved from side to side in the manner of a boatman rowing a small dingy with a single oar. This succeeded in amusing some haymakers who were working in a field close to the railway. As we came down from Cogload flyover I realised that we were going to be overtaken by an express on the down main. Approaching Creech water troughs I shut the regulator and slowed up because I could see what was going to happen. The fireman on the express had his water scoop lowered and as I suspected he managed to overfill his tank. If we had been alongside this engine at this point we would have been drowned in the deluge that poured off of the top of the tender tank.

Chapter Nine

Running Foreman and Controller

Each Friday a parcel of paper books would arrive at the Loco. Department. These were the weekly notices which gave details of engineering work being undertaken on the line, including preparation for track relaying and speed restrictions after the operation had been completed. The track was given a period of 'settling in' following relaying by imposing a speed restriction over the new section, and bridges which had been rebuilt or repaired would be given similar treatment. The booklets were always known as the 'K2 notices'; a pile of these notices was placed beside the signing on point and each driver had to sign to indicate that he had received his copy.

A particular driver named Tom signed on duty and took his copy of the 'K2' notices. On opening it he found that all the pages were blank! For a character such as Tom, who was given to moaning and complaining, this was a heaven sent opportunity to criticise the senior staff for general incompetence. Feedback was almost instantaneous from his colleagues. One told him that it was the management's way of telling him that they knew he was illiterate and another said that he was never given any jobs that required him to go fast enough to comply with a maximum speed limit. There was some irony in the fact that this one blank copy was picked by Tom and he suffered lot of leg pulling over this matter in the ensuing weeks.

Incidents of landslips or localised flooding would warrant a separate notice printed on a single sheet. One such notice that I remember referred to a landslip on an embankment near Wiveliscombe's down distant signal. Heavy rain had brought down the bank on the north side of the line and as this was the only time it had been known to happen, a detailed investigation was made by the district engineer. The farm to the north of the embankment had recently changed hands and the new farmer had ploughed the furrows at right angles to the embankment, whereas his predecessor had always ploughed parallel to the railway. The consequence of this action was that all the water had run down the furrows and had eroded the embankment. The estates department secured an agreement with the farmer to plough parallel to the railway in future and there was no further slippage at this point during the remaining years of the Barnstaple branch.

As a running foreman one got to know the habits and working traits of most men and these became most noticeable to me when I was on night shift. There would be certain men who would sign on about 10 minutes before their booked time and if they were not there by that time you knew they were going to be late and therefore had to rearrange the rosters. If the duty that needed to be covered involved the preparation of the engine you had at least 45 minutes leeway as you could usually find a driver in the cabin who would start this task, but if the driver or fireman was signing on before walking to the station to relieve a train you had to take action immediately.

Such was the case one Saturday morning in the Summer when fireman Ken Rice should have signed on at 3.10 am to work a Paddington-bound train at 3.25

A Mogul stands at the platform at Dulverton with a Barnstaple-Taunton train on 28th September, 1956. The crew have a tarpaulin extended from the cab roof to the tender to obtain a little more protection from the elements.   *H.C. Casserley*

'Castle' class 4-6-0 No. 5056 *Earl of Powis* at Chippenham with an express to Paddington in 1959. The fireman is Clive Bousfield.   *Roger Venning Collection*

am. At 3.20 there was no sign of Ken so I grabbed the fireman who was signing on to work the 4.35 am to Barnstaple and sent him to the station to cover for Ken. I then went to the cabin and found a night turn fireman to start the preparation of the engine for the Barnstaple service. Returning to the office to work out how to cover for Ken's absence, at 3.40 am he turned up at the shed saying he had misread the duty sheet and he now found himself on the 4.35 am to Barnstaple. I saw him again on the following morning and he admitted that he was furious with himself at missing a turn to London and the mileage money that went with it. He said that he was up in good time for the turn and had spent 20 minutes in his garden watering his runner beans.

On another occasion on the night shift I was in the office at about 3.00 am when I had a phone call from the driver on the West Yard shunter saying that his fireman had been injured as a result of the shunter throwing a cup at him. He said that he needed another fireman so I told him to phone me again in 15 minutes. I thought this would give them time to let the situation that had developed settle down, but just in case I looked down my list of firemen and found one who had been on duty since 10 pm who could finish the turn. The phone went again and the driver said that the fireman had gone to hospital for attention to a cut on his head, so I sent my spare fireman to the West Yard. I later had to ask the fireman and the shunter for a written report of this incident. The truth was that the injured fireman had been involved in some horseplay and had made the mistake of teasing the head shunter who was a rather fiery character with a very quick temper. Clearly he had had enough because he had hurled a tea cup at the fireman hitting him on the head. Their written report said that the fireman had been digging coal in the engine's bunker where he had stumbled and had hit his head on the side of the platework.

Even as late as 1961 I can remember special trains being laid on for transatlantic passengers disembarking from liners at Plymouth. This was a legacy of the old rivalry between the Great Western and the London and South Western Railway for the passenger and mail services which dated from before the turn of the century. Although the Salisbury accident and the opening of the 'Berks and Hants' route ended the race up from Plymouth, both the Southern and the Great Western in their post-Grouping period still sought to cultivate this lucrative traffic. Latterly the Southern concentrated upon developing its facilities at Southampton by providing a modern terminal with good passenger facilities and a Pullman train service to Waterloo. The Great Western provided an alternative service from Plymouth in the form of 'tenders' which where small ships that sailed out into Plymouth Sound to collect passengers from transatlantic liners who needed to get up to London in a hurry. The tenders were named after Devonshire 'sea dogs' from the Elizabethan era, the two early vessels being the *Sir Walter Raleigh* and the *Sir Francis Drake*. As late as 1934 the Great Western added two more in the form of the *Sir John Hawkins* and the *Sir Richard Grenville*. The Great Western enjoyed only a brief flirtation with the Pullman Company between 1929 and early 1931. In that year it decided to build a special train comprising eight of the finest carriages ever to grace a British standard gauge railway which became known as the 'Super Saloons'.

As soon as the tender tied up at the Great Western Ocean Terminal the passengers and mail would transfer to the waiting special train. The traffic department was given advanced warning of the number of passengers and also of the likely time of arrival of the liner in Plymouth Sound. Given this information an appropriate number of the 'Super Saloons' would be shunted out of their special accommodation at the rear of Old Oak Common carriage sidings and immediately dispatched to Plymouth. A path would be found for the train ensuring a high speed, non-stop run up to Paddington and Laira Shed would be expected to provide appropriate motive power.

These trains were described by special telegraphic codes; a 'Plym A' being a train of about five 'Super Saloons' weighing about 200 tons hauled by a 'King' class 4-6-0 which would have the tightest point-to-point timings. A 'Plym B' would be a train of the same load headed by a 'Castle' class 4-6-0, a 'Plym C' would be a train of 300 tons with a 'King', while a 'Plym D' would be the same load with a 'Castle'. The timings for such trains was set out in the back pages of the Working Timetables of both the Exeter and Plymouth Divisions. Laira would be expected to provide the best engine possible, often at short notice, and a suitably experienced crew would work straight through to Paddington where they would lodge before returning after a rest period. I never heard of Laira being sent any additional locomotives to cover the working of these trains.

Taunton Shed never had any connection with working this prestige traffic, except on one occasion in 1961 when I was deputising for Mr Aston the shed master. The incident that left a Laira fireman horribly injured when the pricker he was withdrawing from the firebox struck an overbridge was described in Volume One and it occurred while working one of these services. The first news of this accident reached me from the signalman at Cogload who informed me that the driver had taken the train through to Athelney to ensure easy access for the ambulance. I dispatched a Taunton fireman by taxi to Athelney, to work the train on to Paddington with the Laira driver, and then had the task of liaising with the railway's own Welfare Service. This department would ensure that the injured fireman's wife would be contacted and brought to Taunton to be near him while his condition remained critical at East Reach Hospital. My time clerk wished me the best of luck with this unenviable task as he considered that the Welfare Service wasn't up to much. My experience of them proved to be different as they took over completely and handled matters very well. They authorised me to arrange accommodation for his wife which would be convenient to the hospital and I met her off the train and took her by taxi, first to the hospital and later to the lodgings we had found for her. If my memory serves me well the fireman's surname was Kerry and I visited him several times in hospital during what proved to be a long recovery. When his memory and his speech returned he told me that the engine was No. 7029 *Clun Castle* and that the accident had happened because the high front to the Hawksworth tender forced him to raise the handle of the pricker higher than usual in order to get the implement out of the firebox, before sliding it down into the fire-iron tunnel on his side of the footplate.

Later in my career I enquired of Mr Kerry's whereabouts when I was in contact with the foreman at Laira. I was told that he never went back to the footplate and having done various jobs of a light nature for a few years he left the railway. At least the subsequent history of this incident did prove to my time clerk that the Welfare Service did work!

When I began my footplate career Wrong Line Orders were an absolute necessity as a double tracked main line railway was strictly divided into the up line and the down line and were signalled for running in one direction only. Recently many double tracked main lines have been resignalled so that trains can be run in either direction making the Wrong Line Order obsolete. The then universally accepted definition was that the up line was the one on which trains worked towards London and the down line was the one on which trains worked away from the capital, and no running movement could be made in the wrong direction without a Wrong Line Order (WLO). Before any movement in the wrong direction could take place a wrong line order would have to be issued either by a driver, a guard or a signalman. There were four different types of wrong line order form.

The driver carried a green WLO form 'B' (the same colour as his engine) which he would complete and give to his fireman who would walk forward to the signalman at the box in advance, to allow the driver of an assisting engine to come onto the front of his engine, such as in the case of an engine failure.

The guard carried two different types of WLO form, a white one ('C') and a pink one ('A') (the same colour as the lamps on his brake van). The white form would be issued to order the driver set back to rejoin the rear portion of his train in the case of an accidental division. The pink form would be issued by the guard to the signalman in advance when the train had been deliberately divided in cases where the train was overloaded, to allow the engine to return for the rear portion.

The signalman's WLO form 'D' was buff coloured (the same colour as his signal box) and would be issued to a driver permitting him to return to the signal box in the wrong direction in the case, for example, where an engine was waiting to be sent into a section possibly to look for a failed train on the opposite line.

An example of this procedure being used occurred when I was foreman one Sunday afternoon in the Autumn of 1959. I received a message that the diesel locomotive hauling the 1.30 pm Paddington to Plymouth service had failed somewhere in the section between Somerton and Athelney, (at this time of the year the boxes at Curry Rivel Junction and Long Sutton & Pitney were switched out on Sundays). I sent a set of men with a steam locomotive to Athelney with instructions to obtain a WLO from the signalman at Athelney where they were to go into section and find the train. Here they were to get a WLO from the driver of the failed diesel locomotive and return to Athelney using the signalman's WLO. From here they would travel in the wrong direction along the down line with the driver's WLO and couple up to the failed diesel locomotive. The steam engine then hauled this train to Taunton where the failed locomotive was replaced and the traffic proceeded on to its destination.

When an engine failed through being unable to haul its load it inevitably happened on a rising gradient where, in all probability, there would be a catch point or two ahead of the failed engine deliberately placed there to derail vehicles which were running away in the wrong direction. The driver would have to make a note of these on his WLO form before sending his fireman ahead with it. If there was a small signal box without a crossover in the direction in which the fireman would be walking then he would have to get the WLO form countersigned by that signalman also.

In the course of operating the railway many wrong direction movements were made by locomotives engaged in shunting in and around the station. It would have been totally impractical to have completed WLO forms for the multiplicity of shunting movements made during the course of any one day. All of these were carried out under the blanket coverage of movements made within 'station limits'.

All points within the station limits would be signalled by disc signals sometimes these were singles but often doubles or trebles mounted vertically above each other. Sometimes when it was difficult for the driver to observe such signals they might be mounted on a post. Regular movements in the wrong direction would be signalled by a 'backing signal'. Such a signal was quite distinctive in its appearance in that it was half the size of a normal semaphore arm with a rib on its top and bottom edge, painted plain red with no cross band but two holes punched in the arm. These signals were a GWR 'speciality' and did not appear in the standard Rule Book, only the GWR Appendix.

An unusual circumstance arose at Exeter on the up relief line at the west end of the station. Having passed the signal gantry adjacent to Exeter West signal box, which was situated close to the bridge which carried the railway over the River Exe, and being signalled to run into the station on the up relief line, the next signal was the lower arm of two backing signals. It was very unusual arrangement to have a backing signal to run in the right direction! The upper signal would have taken the train in the wrong direction along the down goods loop. The other variety of signal I remember was those used on goods loop lines which were different in having a large white ring attached to the semaphore arm.

On reflection I am sure that locomotive performance would have been much improved if fireman had received a formal training. A cleaner progressing to fireman was responsible for his own learning and could only hope for useful help and guidance from other more experienced firemen. This might happen if he was paired with a senior fireman on shunting duties but you couldn't count upon such chance encounters occurring. Any fool could shovel coal from the bunker and throw it through the firehole door onto the grate, but nobody was charged with the responsibility of explaining the process of combustion to a young fireman. Basic understanding concerning the safe management of boiler water level was tested by inspectors when a cleaner went to be passed for firing duties. However I can't remember any candidate for this exam being questioned about the purpose of the brick arch or the deflector plate which were vital for the complete combustion of the fuel.

Experience taught me that a deflector plate was useless for its intended task when it had been burned back to a length of anything less than 18 inches. It was easy enough for any of us to go to the boilersmith's store and get a new one of the right pattern but too few ever bothered.

If the deflector plate had been properly inserted in the firehole ring the centre line of its underside should align with a point about halfway along the brick arch.

The firehole was protected from possible damage by the shovel and other fire irons by a cast-iron 'shoe' which dropped into place and filled the bottom half of the firehole. This piece had to be fitted first and it was retained in place by its own weight. The deflector plate rested on the shoe and its purpose was to divert the cold air, essential for combustion, down onto the fire and not onto the tubeplate. The problem was that some firemen used to remove the deflector plate deliberately, in order to get more fuel than was necessary into the firebox. This defeated the whole object of this simple but vital piece of equipment and led to many cases of leaking tubes. Firemen working on the British Railways Standard class '9F' 2-10-0s often reverted to this practice in the mistaken belief that the grate couldn't be filled too deeply on these engines! The standard Great Western deflector plates were as follows:

No. 1	All small locomotives including 2-6-0s of the '43XX' class
No. 2	'Kings', 'Castles' and '47XX' class 2-8-0s
No. 3	'Halls', 'Granges', 'Saints', 'Stars', and '28XX' class 2-8-0s
No. 4	'County' class 4-6-0s and LMS '8F' class 2-8-0s

I described how I became a lecturer on the BTC General Railways Course held at Dillington House near Ilminster in Volume One. These courses were run on a two-weekly cycle for railway staff working in a wide range of departments on all the six Regions of British Railways. Each Region sent two members from its Clerical, Operating and Locomotive Departments, and an additional three members were included from Headquarters staff making a total number of 39 attending each course. In the course of the two weeks the course members explored their perceptions of how their various departments worked. They were encouraged to advance their ideas and theories on how their department could best contribute to the efficient operation of the entire railway transport industry.

Having been interviewed by and selected for the post by J.C.L. Palmer, chief training and education officer for BTC, I made a second visit to 222 Marylebone Road, at that time known as the 'Kremlin', about six weeks later. Here I was introduced to Mr Simpson, the Instructor in Charge at Dillington House who arranged for me to meet a number of very senior people within British Railways in order to collect material for my proposed lectures. The dieselisation scheme was then in full swing and the first person I met was Mr J.F. Harrison, chief mechanical engineer of British Railways and President of the Institute of Locomotive Engineers. He was an extremely accommodating but very busy person and I was handed over to his chief assistant Mr Ken Limbert. This gentleman gave me access to all the statistical information I needed on diesel locomotive performance and a dossier detailing the numerous failures that were currently being experienced.

At a Railway Equipment Exhibition that was held at Battersea I was fortunate to be able to have a detailed conversation with a technical representative from Brush Engineering. He missed no opportunity to drive home the success his company had achieved with the marine and electricity generating applications of its diesel engines. He was forced to admit that their installation in railway locomotives had resulted in all sorts of problems that had not attended previous applications. He assured me that the problems being encountered would soon be rectified and the mechanical reliability of the engines fitted to the pilot scheme locomotives would be greatly improved before manufacturers proceeded with batch production. Meanwhile British Railways were running single-engined diesel locomotives in tandem to improve the reliability of this new and untried technology.

I had made copious notes from the information made available to me and from this I prepared a paper showing the effects that dieselisation would have on train working in the future, compared with the then situation of a railway system where 80 per cent of its motive power consisted of steam locomotives. I read my paper to Mr Palmer who listened with interest. He told me that if I was to present this paper to an audience at Dillington I should be careful to state that its conclusions were my own and not the official view of the BTC.

I attended a very intensive course in lecturing skills, at Faverdale Hall near Darlington where I learned the value of careful preparation and the importance of being as good a listener as you were a speaker. I was then presented with the sort of opportunity that many railway enthusiasts of the day would have sold their souls for. I was given leave to visit any railway installation or depot that would assist me to acquire material for my lectures and an 'all Regions' footplate pass, issued with the instruction that I had to give two days' notice of my intention to travel on a specific service. I have already told of my experiences during this period in my earlier book, but the most important issue raised for me was the wide variation of recognised practice covered by agreements negotiated through Local Departmental Committees.

My first weeks as a lecturer were a period of great nervous tension, but the opportunity to join in with the discussion groups that followed was a time for me to assess the effectiveness of my input and was usually reassuring enough for me to recover my self confidence. As these courses were intended to provide opportunities for each railway department to appreciate the problems of the others it was important to avoid jargon or slang phrases. Having a heritage stretching back for a century and a half there were many words that had been assimilated into the working vocabulary of the industry. This was brought home to me early in the course of my lectureship when a clerical officer asked me to explain the terms 'dummy' and 'board' that had been used by Loco. Department personnel during the course of our discussion group.

The Warden of Dillington House was a Mr Harvey-Sheppard who presented some lectures on the theme of human relationships in the work place. He provided some very thought provoking material on the effects of the significant number of immigrants who were being recruited to work in this industry. Our discussions, now over 30 years ago, revealed a refreshingly modern and enlightened attitude to the employment of people from ethnic minority groups. The lecture room at Dillington House had a wonderful Adams fireplace on either side of which were two wonderfully carved statues in white marble depicting naked females. During the course of one of his lectures Mr Harvey-Sheppard noticed that a student was being distracted by these two figures whereupon he stopped and asked the student what was fascinating him? The student said he wondered what the statues were supposed to represent to which Mr Harvey- Sheppard replied immediately 'Seniority and Suitability'.

While I was at Dillington House I learned a lot more about railway traffic matters. One particular problem arose during the conveyance of glass which we can all appreciate is a very fragile material. While the railway had learned from experience a variety of successful methods to ensure that it wasn't damaged in transit it had never really overcome the problem of ensuring that it remained dry. If moisture managed to penetrate between large sheets of glass air pressure resulted in them becoming inseparable.

I was interested by the new 'Polybulk' system that was being introduced for the conveyance of cement powder in bulk form. In the new wagons the cement powder could be pumped out from a valve in the base by admitting compressed air to the container. This system was later adapted for the china clay traffic which originated in Cornwall. Huge 100 tonne 'Polybulk' tank wagons were constructed with a central membrane running the entire length of the tank. China clay powder would be loaded on the right hand side of the flexible screen and a train of these wagons would travel from this country to Italy via the Cross-Channel train ferry. The wagons would be discharged and sent to Austria where they would be loaded with grain on the other side of the screen. The wagons would return to this country, again via Dover, and travel to Exeter where the grain would be discharged into large storage silos. As soon as the 'Polybulk' wagons had been discharged they were dispatched to Cornwall for reloading with china clay powder and back on the circuit to Italy and Austria.

Rail-borne containers were nothing new because the GWR had been using them since the 1930s. The clean white-painted insulated meat containers were used on the regular train which left Lloyd Maunder's siding at Tiverton Junction each evening at around 5.30 pm, conveying meat for Smithfield Market in London.

Containers were adapted to convey a variety of rail traffic and around about 1955 somebody came up with the brilliant idea of a folding, collapsible container fabricated from light alloys. These were made in variety of sizes from the original standard variety down to one which only had a capacity of about 10 cubic feet. When the container had been discharged it would be folded down to a flat pack and about 10 of these could be fitted inside one erect container for return to a central depot. The new folding containers were called 'Colicos' but their early success led to their rapid downfall as traders receiving them recognised their value and failed to return them.

The British Railways Modernisation plan of the mid-1950s saw the gradual introduction of a range of widely differing diesel locomotives on the national network. With the arrival of diesel shunting locomotives at Taunton in the Spring of 1960, a number of our fitters attended courses to teach them the new skills needed to keep these engines running. The diesel locomotives allocated to Taunton were 0-6-0 diesel mechanical units that had been built at Swindon. They were fitted with a Gardner 8L3 engine rated at 204 hp and were capable of a theoretical top speed of 28 mph. They were numbered D2134, D2140 and D2142. Two of these locomotives were immediately deployed in the yards at Taunton and one was outstabled at Bridgwater. One of the locomotives regularly worked the 7.10 freight to Dunball. Among the problems these locomotives created for me as a foreman was that when we had a '57XX' 0-6-0

'D63XX' class B-B enters Bristol Temple Meads on an up freight on 5th January, 1963. *Exe Rail*

Double-headed 'Hymeks' Nos. D7012 and D7040 provide the motive power for this passenger train at Taunton on 1st September, 1962.   *C.L. Caddy*

pannier tank shunting in the yard on weekdays it was versatile enough to run a passenger train to Chard, Yeovil or Minehead. This work was out of the question for our diesel shunters. These engines were reclassified class '03' several years later and had their numbers adjusted accordingly. It wasn't until May 1962 that we were allocated our first diesel electric shunting locomotive numbered D4163 (later class '08'). This was significantly more powerful than the 'D21XX' series we were originally allocated and it too settled down to a hum-drum existence in the yards.

My duties as a running foreman during this period were not always confined to activities going on around the shed. I also had to look out for men signing on to relieve main line trains and also the replacement of locomotives that had failed or developed a fault. With the introduction of main line diesel locomotives I also had to be aware if the men waiting to relieve a train had been passed out on the class of diesel locomotive that might be hauling it.

Four Taunton drivers had been sent on a comprehensive course to learn how to operate all the diesel locomotives that were being introduced on the Western Region. They became 'tutor drivers' and would accompany the normal crew on turns where a diesel locomotive had been diagrammed. The dates for the introduction of these classes were as follows:

The North British Loco. Co. 2,000 hp AIA-AIA 'D600' 'Warship' Series in February 1958
The BR Swindon/North British 2,100/2,200 hp B-B 'D800' 'Warship' class, (class '42/43') in August 1958
The North British Loco. Co. 1,000/1,100 hp B-B 'D63XX' (class '22') in January 1959
The Beyer, Peacock (Hymek) Ltd 1,700 hp B-B 'D70XX', (class '35') in May 1961
The BR Swindon/Crewe 2,700 hp 'Western' class 'D10XX' (class '52') in December 1961

When the 'D70XX' type '3'diesel-hydraulic locomotives, known to all as the 'Hymeks', were introduced in 1961 they were deployed on such duties as would have been covered by the '49XX' and '68XX' class 4-6-0s. Their first regular appearance at Taunton was when two, working in multiple, would arrive with the 12.30 am freight from Bristol, West Depot. On arrival at the shed we would separate them and the Bristol crew would take one of them to work the 6.35 am passenger service to Temple Meads. The other one would remain for driver training and then work the 10.20 am passenger service to Minehead and return, before retracing its steps to Bristol with the 1.30 pm stopping train.

One morning in the early 1960s Reg Aston, the shed master, asked me if my work was all up to date and when I assured him that it was, he suggested that I might like to ride on the 'D7000' 'Hymek' that would be on the 10.20 am Taunton to Minehead service. I enjoyed my trip but I soon realised that you were driving by instruments as you didn't sense the speed at which you were travelling as you did on a steam engine.

The winter created a fresh set of problems for our growing fleet of diesel locomotives in that the train heating boilers proved less than reliable. It became common practice to couple a steam locomotive behind the diesel locomotive just to provide steam to heat the carriages. This was doubly wasteful as besides the additional fuel used on the steam locomotive there was also the logistical problem of having to find a second set of men. Even when we had found a set

'D800' 'Warship' class B-B No. D830 *Majestic* pulls away from Exeter St David's on an up train on 10th July, 1962. *H.C. Casserley*

'Western' class C-C No. D1003 *Western Pioneer* is seen on a down passenger train at Exeter St David's on 10th July, 1962. *H.C. Casserley*

of men and a steam locomotive to heat a train arriving at Taunton behind a diesel locomotive with a failed train heating boiler there were additional delays. Operating orders ruled that the steam locomotive had to be coupled behind the diesel, because it was feared that coal dislodged from the steam engine's tender would smash the diesel locomotive's windscreen and hot ashes from the steam locomotive's chimney might be sucked into the diesel cooling system.

The first of the new main line diesel hydraulic locomotives introduced under the pilot scheme for the Western Region were the five type '4' 'D600' series of the 'Warship' class. These locomotives were built by the North British Locomotive Company of Glasgow and were equipped with MAN diesel engines and Voith hydraulic transmissions. They were rated at 2,000 hp and the locomotive was carried on a pair of six-wheeled bogies with only the outer axles driven, the centre one being a load bearing idler. These gradually made their appearance from February 1958 and within six months had taken over the haulage of such prestigious trains as the 'Cornish Riviera Express'. Their introduction was attended with many teething problems and within a comparatively short time they had been completely eclipsed by the more numerous members of the 'D800' 'Warship' class. With the later introduction of the 'D1000' 'Western' class these five locomotives were soon displaced from the principal express passenger trains and were all transferred to Laira, where they were used on semi-fast services in Cornwall and the china clay traffic.

By the mid-1960s the only regular appearance they made north of Plymouth was on an express goods service which ran each afternoon between Newton Abbot and Bristol, on which the first scheduled stop was at Bridgwater.

On one occasion the train arrived at Bridgwater and ran up the goods loop where the locomotive stopped opposite the signal box. It hadn't been stopped for more than a minute or two when there was a huge explosion when an accumulation of gas ignited in the four large batteries. The force of the blast was such that the side covers of the battery boxes, which where 1 in. thick, 4 ft long and 3 ft wide , were hurled right across the main line and smashed into the lower half of the signal box. Although every window in the box was smashed by the blast the only human casualty was the unfortunate signalman, who spent the next three days in the local hospital suffering from shock. The train which consisted of eight wagons was shunted into the yard and D604 *Cossack* was pushed up to the dead end of the headshunt to await collection.

The advanced technology of the new diesel locomotives caused quite a few headaches for anybody involved with their operation. Having worked a freight service from Newton Abbot to Taunton a 'D800' series 'Warship' locomotive would come to shed and wait in a siding before working the 7.50 am Taunton to Weston-super-Mare passenger service. On this particular morning the crew for this turn found that they couldn't start the engine. Hurriedly I had to find a steam locomotive and a set of men to work the 7.50 am service. There was no tender locomotive available but I was able to find BR Standard class '3' 2-6-2T No. 82030. I also instructed them that they were to return directly to Taunton with this locomotive as it was needed for the 9.30 am Chard freight. Having made these arrangements I went to find what the problem was with 'Warship' class D806 *Cambrian*. It subsequently transpired that the locomotive had been

'Warship' class No. D848 *Sultan* on the 'Devonian' at Taunton on 13th June, 1964.

C.L. Caddy

visited by a fitter who had been given instructions to run up the engine to check on any possible faults. He entered the cab at the Exeter end and instead of taking the proper operating handle he used a spanner on the stub of the reversing control. When he shut the engine down he had removed his spanner from the reversing control without returning it to the neutral position. This had prevented the engine from starting. By the time I had got the fitter to sort out the problem he had created it was too late for the locomotive to work the 7.50 am service and so the crew took D806 light engine to Bristol, Bath Road Shed.

While researching material for my lectures at Dillington House I was privileged to have been able to spend a couple of days at the Railway Technical College at Derby. One of the departments I visited was the diesel training centre where fitters were trained to work on the new locomotives. As with all such brief encounters it is impossible to absorb and fully comprehend everything you were shown, but one piece of equipment that caught my eye was an appliance for testing for faults in the vacuum brake system fitted to either the locomotive or the rolling stock. This consisted of a metal tube about 1 ft long with a train pipe flexible vacuum hose fitted at each end. In the centre of the pipe was a hand operated valve which could isolate either end and on either side of the valve was a vacuum gauge. Months after this visit to Derby I was in the stores back at Taunton and to my surprise I found that we had been allocated one of these pieces of equipment. With diesel-hydraulic locomotives now being used on freight trains problems had arisen because they lacked the weight to give them adequate braking power to handle a loose coupled, unfitted freight train. An order went out that they could not work a freight train unless it contained at least 10 vacuum braked wagons coupled immediately behind the engine.

I was on late turn one week when the 'D800' class diesel locomotive working the Bristol to Hackney Yard (Newton Abbot) freight train failed in the East Yard at Taunton. The freight yard foreman phoned me to say that the train was stuck because the locomotive couldn't blow the brakes off. On a 'D800' class locomotive a fail safe device prevented the power handle being used until the locomotive had created a vacuum of 25 inches in the system. Here was an opportunity to use the vacuum brake testing equipment that we had in the stores, so collecting this piece of kit and my diesel fitter, I told my timekeeper we were off to the East Yard.

Here we found D816 *Eclipse* and the driver explained to me that the vacuum exhauster was running continuously, indicating that there was a serious leak in the system, and the wagon examiners had already checked the train and had assured him that there was no leakage there. Watched by the examiners I instructed my fitter to connect our piece of equipment to the   vacuum pipes between the locomotive and the first wagon. The exhauster was kept running and the isolating handle on the equipment was placed in the open position and we watched while the gauges crept up to 20 inches. I then told the fitter to close the central valve isolating the locomotive vacuum pipe from the train vacuum pipe. Now the gauge on the locomotive side rose rapidly to 25 inches while the gauge on the train side dropped to zero. I pointed out to the traffic inspector that there was a bad leak on the train and as soon as this was rectified the

'Western' class No. D1001 *Western Pathfinder* in maroon livery at Taunton on 8th September, 1962.   *C.L. Caddy*

Two 'Westerns' sporting different liveries at Taunton on 13th June, 1964. D1015 *Western Champion* (*left*) is in ochre, while D1002 *Western Explorer* is green. Both have had yellow warning panels painted around their headcode boxes.   *C.L. Caddy*

locomotive would be all right. Soon after we arrived back at the shed from the East Yard I saw D816 heading towards Exeter on the goods loop. Obviously someone must have rectified the fault on the wagons.

As a running foreman I was given no information about the operation of the 'D7000' 'Hymek' class locomotives and found myself gleaning whatever I could from tutor drivers and fitters. I quickly discovered that the two cabs were named 'A' end and 'B' end but were different in that the 'A' cab contained a console with all the control relays in it and on the side of the console was a panel with fault indicator lights which glowed either red or blue. The fault lights indicated 'low water level', 'low water temperature', 'oil level', 'oil temperature', etc., and the convention was that a blue light indicated everything was normal but a red light was a warning. There was also a 'general alarm' light which would turn red if any of the fault indicator lights turned red. The 'B' cab only had a 'general alarm' fault indicator light fitted to it, the console not being fitted at this end. The most common fault indicator to turn red was the 'low water temperature' warning light which occurred if the engine had been standing idle for more than about two hours without its pre-heaters switched on. If a driver attempted to start the engine from the 'B' end and the 'general alarm' light came up he would have to go to the 'A' end to identify where the problem was.

On the side of the console was the semi-rotary-switch which was marked 'TRAFFIC/SHUNT'. If the switch was left in the 'SHUNT' position it locked out No. 1 gear to avoid the mechanism changing from No. 1 gear to No. 2 gear and back again while carrying out slow shunting movements. If it was in the other 'TRAFFIC' position it would change up to second gear as soon as the speed reached about 7 mph. One thing I quickly learned was that if the 'low water temperature' fault indicator light was shining it was possible to open the glass door on the console and lift the armature of the water temperature relay with a piece of wood the size of a pencil causing the warning light to turn blue which would permit the engine to start. Once started the engine would remain running, and the water temperature light would turn blue as would the 'general alarm' light. This was all highly irregular but it got us out of trouble on more than one occasion.

In 1963 problems began to be experienced with the Mekydro transmissions fitted to the 'Hymek' that had been built under licence in this country by Stone. As an experiment the odd numbered members of the class had their engine power derated and the even numbered locomotives had their No. 1 gear isolated. The whole class ran in this condition for over a year while modifications were made to certain components. I was on night shift as traction controller at Bristol during the time that the problems with these locomotives began to be resolved. The Avonmouth area traffic controller called across to me to report that the driver of the 10.30 pm Avonmouth to Exeter freight had a faulty locomotive. Knowing that the locomotive allocated to this turn was D7068 I doubted that there was any real problem and so I spoke to the traffic inspector. He said that the locomotive would not lift the load as No. 1 gear had been locked out. I knew that by then all the 'Hymeks' had been restored to their original settings so I asked the inspector to approach the driver in as diplomatic a way as possible to check the position of the 'TRAFFIC/SHUNT' switch on the side of the console in the 'A' end cab. After about 10 minutes the Avonmouth controller called across to say that the 10.30 pm Avonmouth to Exeter was on its way. It seems strange to me that if I had not picked up this little bit of knowledge unofficially I would have been powerless to prevent an unnecessary delay. As I continued to work at this job I realised I had to have a wide range of technical knowledge, a lot of common sense and an element of ingenuity to get by.

I had become steam engine controller at Bristol during the final phase of steam operation in the Bristol area and within six months of my appointment the steam engine control desk had closed. However brief this period was I do feel that I made my mark during this time, particularly over the matter of the engine allocation sheets.

The 9.15 am Bristol West Depot to Water Orton was a diesel turn while the 9.50 am Bristol West Depot to Washwood Heath remained a steam-hauled turn. I remember that I had allocated the locomotive for this latter turn one morning when the deputy chief controller came over and rubbed out the engine number for the 9.50 am train and wrote 'Caped [Cancelled], No Power' and then reallocated my steam locomotive to the 9.15 am West Depot to Water Orton turn. I was hopping mad about this and rubbed out his comment regarding the availability of power for the 9.50 am service. Here I added my own comment in red ink, 'Cancelled, Steam Locomotive taken to cover the failure of Diesel Locomotive on 9.15 am to Water Orton'. At about 11.00 am Mr Griffiths, the chief controller, came down to inspect the allocation sheets before attending his midday conference with headquarters staff. When he saw my comments he was furious that I had dared to suggest that the new motive power was anything short of perfect. I stuck to my guns and came back at him that the deputy chief controller was depriving me of steam locomotives to cover for the poor availability of the diesel locomotives! The outcome of this was that in future the deputy chief controller had to liaise more closely with me if steam engines were needed to cover for the diesel locomotives.

With the demise of regular steam locomotive workings in the Bristol area I was absorbed into the office complex and was placed on the Worcester traffic desk. This was something completely new for me as I was working with traffic inspectors, guards and engine crews. Early in this period I noticed from the stock sheets that there had been an inexplicable build up in 'vanfits' (four-wheeled, vacuum fitted freight vans) in the yards around Worcester. I phoned Hector the yard inspector and asked him if he could explain this situation. He told me that 'catalogue time' was coming up and as soon as he had the word from Messrs Kays, the large Worcester-based mail order company, he would be using them. This was a huge operation with fleets of lorries bringing the new catalogues to the station for dispatch all over the country. Every train approaching Worcester would be routed into the yard to attach the loaded vanfits up to the maximum weight permitted. As the number of empty vans in the Worcester yards diminished, local trip workings brought in more vans from the outlying sidings at Evesham and Honeybourne for loading. While this rush was on we still had to maintain the same level of service to our regular customers, the largest of these being the inward traffic of sheet tin plate for the

Metal Box Company and empty open wagons needed for their scrap material. This job afforded me a wider picture of the work of the railway than the Motive Power Department had ever done.

At the same time as managing the flow of this traffic I had to keep an eye on the progress of passenger trains through the area. These generally had priority over freight trains but it was important to regulate all movements by the headcode allocated to each train. I had to work closely with Norton Junction where the Western Region line from Oxford converged with the short link line from the Midland Region main line from Gloucester to Birmingham. The next signal box at the other end of the link from the Midland route was Abbotswood Junction. If Norton Junction had a train standing there and was not able to take a following train from Abbotswood Junction for the Worcester route all traffic towards Birmingham on the Midland Region route came to a stop.

I arrived at work one morning to find that I had a 'D800' class and a 'D7000' class both at Oxford and nobody could find me a set of men to bring them to Bristol for repair. I phoned my old shed master at Taunton who confirmed he had a spare set of men who were familiar with 'D800' locomotives. I told him to have them travel on the 9.15 am train from Taunton to Reading where they would change for Oxford. In the meantime Swindon found me a spare driver so I asked for him to be sent to Oxford to pilot the Taunton men when they arrived. With the Taunton men operating the 'D800' on one engine they towed the failed 'Hymek' back to Bristol for immediate repair. Both locomotives had already been out of service for two days and if I hadn't come up with a solution as to how to move them they might still have been at Oxford a week later.

Even with the introduction of the new diesel-hydraulic locomotives the Western Region continued to make use of the old GWR Automatic Train Control system whose origins lay in the early years of the century. The appearance of Midland Region diesel-electric locomotives on the Western Region raised a problem because these were equipped with the British Railways Automatic Warning System, which was not compatible with the earlier system. The unions had been pressing hard for the fitting of ATC to all these locomotives prior to their introduction on the Western Region, but as the scheme to replace this equipment with the British Railways AWS was well in hand nothing was done. This decision contributed to an accident at Bridgwater in the early 1970s. At 1.00 am a block train of fertilizer from Ince & Elton had arrived at Bridgwater and was standing on the down main line waiting to be shunted into the up sidings from the east end.

Meanwhile the 6.39 pm express freight from Derby to Exeter hauled by a Midland Region diesel-electric locomotive was speeding down the track from Bristol. Neither the driver nor the secondman of this train had noticed a colour light signal showing 'yellow' and with no ATC siren to warn them, they collided with the back of the stationary train. The guard of the Derby train was riding in the rear cab of the diesel-electric locomotive as there was no brake van on the train. The first wagon next to the engine was a 16 ton mineral wagon loaded with coal and in the collision this was up-ended and its contents emptied into the rear cab burying the poor guard. The accident report concluded that both driver and secondman were asleep.

The emergency services raised a Red Alert when someone realised that the spilled diesel oil from the ruptured fuel tank on the locomotive and the fertilizer in the damaged wagons could mix to form the ingredients of a huge bomb. People living near the scene of the accident had to be evacuated from their homes and it was nearly a week before the scene of the accident was completely cleared.

The union ASLEF used this accident to illustrate their concern for the need for AWS to be extended to all Regions of British Railways and the demise of the older, but equally effective, Western Region ATC was accelerated.

Work began on the building of the M5 motorway at about this time. This resulted in pulverised fuel ash (PFA or 'fly ash') being transported from South Wales to the construction site to consolidate the bed of the road where it ran over the soft peat of the Somerset Levels. Train loads of PFA ran from Aberthaw in South Wales to specially constructed sidings at Puxton. The sidings were located adjacent to the up side of the line between the site of Puxton & Worle station and Yatton. They were inclined upwards and ran on an embankment to a point where the contents of the hopper wagons could be discharged directly into lorries waiting underneath. Each train consisted of about 35 wagons and was hauled by two class '37' diesel-electric locomotives. They ran direct from Aberthaw to Weston-super-Mare where the locomotives ran around their train and proceeded back up the main line and then reversed into the sidings for discharging.

The class '37' diesel-electric locomotives were based in South Wales and no fitters or drivers based on the Bristol side of the Severn tunnel had any knowledge of the type. Generally we just hoped and prayed that nothing would go wrong with these locomotives while they were under our control but then one night I had a problem. The driver of an empty 'fly ash' train phoned Control from Puxton to say he was worried because one of his pair of class '37s' was low on fuel. This might have been an oversight at the locomotive's home depot or it might indicate a fuel leak or engine fault. Either way we didn't have the capability to rectify it at Bath Road Depot and I had to come up with a quick solution to this problem. After a few moments' thought I instructed the driver to shut down the locomotive which was low on fuel and haul it and the 35 empty wagons back to Newport. Having concern that this heavy train might cause problems in the Severn tunnel, I further suggested that he stop at Pilning and restart the second engine to give him the extra power to climb the steep grade to Severn Tunnel Junction. As I never heard any more I assume my suggestion had succeeded in resolving this tricky situation.

Appendix One

Wellington
by P.H. Grant

When describing his footplate career, Jack Gardner frequently refers to the Wellington Bankers. I look at them from another perspective. They were an everyday part of the scene throughout my trainspotting days at Wellington. Jack Gardner also speaks of Mr J.E. James, the senior foreman at Taunton Shed. He, too, was part of my trainspotting days, from their very beginning. Mr James was my grandfather. He retired in June 1943 after 49½ years service with the Great Western Railway, 20 of them in the foreman's post at Taunton. Incidentally, his successor, Reg Aston, was then in charge for 21 years until the shed closed to steam in October 1964.

My grandfather became a widower in 1946 and came to live with us in Wellington soon afterwards. He became person-in-charge of my perambulator but, so far as I recall, we signed for only two routes from home in Owen Street. One was to the station and the other to the nearby 'Basins', Fox's Factory reservoirs adjoining the railway line between Linden Bridge and Westford footpath level crossing (nowadays protected by miniature warning lights).

Throughout most of the 1940s and into the early 1950s, Taunton Shed had a regular allocation of four '51XX' class engines, largely for banking duties. These were Nos. 4113, 4117, 4136 and 5172. In earlier times, '3150' class engines were used as bankers - an ideal engine for such duties, weighing over 81 tons. But, at Taunton, this became a serious drawback from when '51XX' class engines were authorised over the Minehead branch in the late 1930s. Being 'red' engines, the '3150' class was confined to main line local work, banking duties and passenger pilot duties (at Taunton station). So they were displaced by the '51XX' class at Taunton. Nevertheless, the '3150' class engines enjoyed a remarkable longevity on banking duties at Sapperton (Gloucester engines), in South Devon (Laira engines) and in the Severn tunnel especially (Severn Tunnel Junction engines). The last survivor, No. 3170 was broken up in 1961 in Woodham's Yard, at Barry. If the last batch of '51XX' class engines had survived as long, they would still have been in service in the year 2000.

Over the years, 10 o'clock was the regular morning changeover time for the Wellington Banker. When in repose (which was often the case during the day-time except on Summer Saturdays), the banker was normally stabled in one of two places. The first was in the up passenger platform loop, opposite the waiting room but far enough along from the signal box (which was also on this platform), to avoid affecting the signalman's view of passing trains. This was convenient because, on return from Whiteball, the engine would normally take water from the column at the Exeter end of this platform. When this was finished, the engine would gently move along the platform to its spot and the crew adjourn to the signal box. The loop was rarely used for regulating purposes but, of course, had to be clear at certain times of the day for the infrequent Exeter-Taunton stopping passenger service. So, more often than not, the banker would saunter off light engine to Taunton sometime after 9.30 am, departing from the loop. If, however, it had immediately previously been up to Whiteball, it would dash through Wellington, on return, making those swheesh-swheesh, swheesh-shweesh noises, so characteristic of those engines.

The manner by which its replacement arrived from Taunton varied from day to day. Normally, it arrived light engine, pausing on the down main line for the signalman to reverse the points enabling it to set back to the other usual place of repose - just inside the down refuge siding, adjacent to the goods yard. Three short blasts would be given on the whistle to indicate clear of all running lines and repose commenced. However, there were occasions when a down freight, needing assistance to Whiteball, was ready to leave

'Castle' class 4-6-0 No. 5028 *Llantilio Castle* with a down express climbing Wellington bank on 29th March, 1948.

Pursey Short

Taunton at around changeover time. The banker was then attached at Taunton and continued through to Whiteball. Because of the undulating gradients, the banker was coupled in rear as far as Wellington where the train would stop specially to uncouple the banker before continuing to Whiteball. In the case of a passenger or parcels (etc.) train needing such assistance from Taunton, the banker would be coupled at the front of the train, and ahead of the main engine.

There were places where it was necessary to couple the banker inside the main engine (i.e. between it and the train); this was also dependent on the wheel arrangement of the banking engine. These instructions were set down in the Regional Appendix. But, at Wellington, a '51XX' class engine was permitted to be coupled ahead of any class of engine except a '60XX' ('King') class engine. This could give rise to the splendid spectacle of No. 5172 (or one of its confreres) forging through Wellington at the head of a down express, exhibiting a class 'A' headcode. To reduce delays, this configuration would normally continue to Burlescombe (rather than Whiteball) where the banker was detached. It was more common to see this at the 5.00 pm changeover time. The only down express normally around at 10.00 am was the 5.30 am Paddington-Plymouth (reporting number 100) which was booked to call at Wellington and, on Tuesdays only, at Tiverton Junction. It was occasionally banked from Wellington.

Digressing from bankers, there was another daily event after the passage of the 5.30 am Paddington-Plymouth. The booking clerk would leave his office at this time and walk along the platform to pay a call. He was a cheery soul with a distinctive side-to-side gait, rather like a '43XX' class engine when starting. 'Good morning lads', he would call out and then add, for example, 'Fifty-fifty, Earl of St Germans'. And, of course, the next up train, the Plymouth-Liverpool (Lime Street) express would produce the said No. 5050. This was a Shrewsbury engine, always immaculate, working the second half of their double-home turn to Newton Abbot. This ploy was infallible three days a week; on the others, it was a Newton Abbot engine, neither as immaculate nor as predictable. Shrewsbury maintained the same engine in the working for weeks at a time; one can readily recall Nos. 5097 *Sarum Castle*, 5038 *Morlais Castle* and 1016 *County of Hants*, as well as old 5050, at various times.

By mid-morning, one, maybe two, down goods trains would have stopped for assistance. On still days, one could hear a plodding '28XX' or '43XX' class engine labouring up the gradient between Poole Siding and Smith's bridge. On passing the down home signal, steam would be shut off and the blower opened. The whole enterprise would shuffle to a halt at the down starting signal (or down platform starting signal if another train was closely following). As the banker approached, the guard would dismount and hand up to the fireman a note of the train load and engine number, together with any relevant pleasantries. He then repaired to his van, gave a wave of the arm as a Ready to Start signal, released the handbrake and, finally, removed the tail lamp (but not the side lamps). Once on the move, he generally retreated to his 'office', closing the door behind him.

We spotters generally observed this part of the proceedings from the Exeter end of the station. If the signal was cleared, the banker would give two 'crows' on the whistle (there was a certain artistry in this performance) and, as soon as steam could be seen rising from the train engine returning these 'crows' the banker was off. In later years especially, the bank engines were past their best and steam would escape from every pore, but they did their share of the work as could be seen by the wagons being buffered up well towards the front of the train.

Many years later, I asked a group of traction inspectors to define precisely what is meant by a 'crow' and where had it been laid down in the rules, regulations and instructions. It was not defined in the Rule Book of the day. The consensus was that a 'crow' on the whistle should resemble the morning call of the cockerel. Something like one long and four short blasts (or maybe two pairs of short blasts). No-one knew of the existence of a precise definition.

The departure of the of the banker effectively deprived Wellington of cover for 25 to 30 minutes depending on progress up the hill and finding a margin to return light engine. Seven minutes was the return allowance (i.e. the *minimum* time, not to be reduced) for '51XX' class engines and eight minutes for other classes. In addition, water would need to be taken after every second trip; it was routinely taken after each trip unless a train was waiting.

The second day-time changeover time for the banker was at 5.00 pm. About an hour before this, a '49XX' or '68XX' class engine used to arrive, tender-first, from Taunton, together with a passenger brakevan. In due course, this formed the 5.55 pm Wellington to West Ealing milk train (this time and destination varied as the years passed). The milk was brought through the main streets of Wellington from Aplin & Barrett's plant in Mantle Street. Until the early 1950s, it was conveyed in road/rail tanks which were hauled on (and off) the flat wagons by a system of pulleys and cables connected to the tractor bringing them to the station. This took place in the dock at the Exeter end of the down platform. Milk traffic was passenger-rated so the train and its working were presided over by a passenger guard, but the duties which involved getting hands dirty were undertaken by the shunter at Wellington. The engine and van arrived in the down platform and, after a decent interval for pleasantries (there used to be a lot of this), proceeded to the dock siding, attached the loaded flats, placed them in the down platform, ran round and in very much due course, departed under the control of the ground disc signal leading to the up line. From about 1953, the milk was brought by road tanker and pumped into 3,000 gallon rail tanks, using the dock at the Taunton end of the down platform. The train arrangements were much as before.

Normally about three to five tanks were dispatched daily, the train picking up at Puxton & Worle until that traffic was lost to rail in 1955. The bankers did not normally sully themselves with this working except, in certain years, on Summer Saturdays. Tanks from Hemyock were attached at Tiverton Junction to the rear of the late afternoon Exeter-Taunton stopping passenger train. The banker was then used to retrieve these from the rear on arrival at Wellington and shunt them onto the milk train proper. Having left Hemyock at 3.00 pm, these tanks were, as the crow flies, no nearer London at 6.00 pm than at the outset. In fact they had been in transit for 3 hours, averaging 5 mph! In other years, the milk train started from Tiverton Junction on Summer Saturdays, the engine and van going directly there from Taunton, and calling at Wellington to pick up on the return. In all cases, the working was the preserve of a Taunton '49XX' or '68XX'.

There was further action at around tea-time on Mondays to Fridays. This was the arrival of the 'Banbury', the 4.40 pm Taunton-Wellington class 'K' freight. It was almost always worked by a Taunton '57XX' class engine, arriving bunker first with between five and 15 wagons, generally speaking. This mostly comprised coal for William Thomas, who had a private siding adjacent to the station, and conflats with empty BD containers for Price Brothers, who forwarded furniture/bedding traffic. They had a factory in South Street. To a small boy, it was an alarming sight to see these huge wooden caskets (BD containers) making wobbly progress on a trailer hauled by a Thornycroft tractor unit through the town centre. They looked no more stable than Gladys Emmanuel on the district nurse's bike.

The 'Banbury' produced two most unusual engines sometime in the early 1950s. Firstly, there was '94XX' class engine No. 8413, nearly brand new, from Bristol St Philip's Marsh. Jack Gardner relates in his earlier book the brief allocation when new of No. 8456 to Taunton. Being a 'red' engine, it was of only limited use at Taunton and, after only a few weeks, it was exchanged with Exeter's '57XX' class engine No. 9646. The other oddity was '90XX' class engine No. 9008, then a Swindon engine. These were never common at Wellington, even less so in the sidings there. For several weeks in early 1958, the working was brightened up with '22XX' class No. 2230 (a Taunton engine recently transferred from Exeter). This was resplendent in fresh lined green livery following a visit to Newton Abbot works. The 'Banbury' was scheduled to return to Taunton (West Yard) at 6.20 pm.

The highlight of trainspotting days at Wellington was, without doubt, Summer Saturdays, especially in the mid and late 1950s. Attention naturally focussed on the down line. In the other direction, trains passed unchecked in much the same manner, whether hauled by a 'King' class engine or a '43XX' class, and whether comprising eight or 14 vehicles. As a rule, two bank engines were provided, sometimes three. Generally, one was stabled in the down refuge siding and the other(s) alongside in the goods yard. They still returned from Whiteball via the up platform loop in order to take water, but the first available margin would be used to cross the engine to the down refuge siding or yard.

Many trains, of course, did not need assistance but there was a tendency, once a train had stopped for that purpose, for the next train to take assistance as well. If closely following departures had been made from Taunton, it was inevitable that the second train would be delayed by the previous train being banked. It would often be several trains (indeed, sometimes many trains) later before it became possible to achieve a clear run. Having passed Wellington's down distant signal at caution, drivers would immediately shut off steam and come slowly from signal to signal. As soon as the previous train cleared the overlap of the Intermediate Block Section home signal, the signalman would clear the signals as quickly as possible and, if a train was approaching the signal box, he would go to the window and vigorously wave his lever cloth up and down. This usually resulted in a touch on the whistle followed by that familiar 'phutt' as the regulator was opened. What followed is what steam is all about. Maybe it was a familiar Laira 'Castle' class engine or a leaky old '43XX' class engine from Banbury or Pontypool Road; drivers would really go for it, taking a charge at the bank before encountering the steepest part beyond Wellington. Hence the expression - 'to give it some welly'! Alternatively, the driver would give several touches on the whistle or ignore the handsignal altogether, which meant to say: 'Yes, I've seen your duster but I'm still stopping'.

If there was then no banker available and the following train was in the offing, this would pass through the down platform loop. This in itself meant delay, with the distant signal locked at caution and the train checked to the down inner home signal and then 15 mph maximum over the loop entrance and exit points. If that train also needed assistance, the delays really piled up. The maximum permitted loads for passenger trains unassisted from Wellington to Whiteball were as follows:

'King' class	485 tons
'Castle' class	450 tons
'47XX' class	435 tons
'Hall' class	420 tons
'Grange' class	420 tons
'43XX' class	394 tons

But these were really somewhat academic. What stopped, or did not stop, for assistance was frequently a matter of surprise. Much depended on the steaming state of the engine, the state of mind of the crew, whether a clear run was available, whether the banker was on hand and, not least, the weather. A mild West Country drizzle made a lot of difference.

Much has been written about engine working on Summer Saturdays so mention is made here of a few highlights. The day's biggest cheer was reserved for the '47XX' class 2-8-0 engines. Three or four would be seen on a good Saturday. In earlier years, '28XX' and '43XX' class engines also played their part but the 2-8-0s were eclipsed by the BR Standard '9F' class engines. From the spotting viewpoint, one of Birkenhead's four 'Grange' class engines (Nos. 6831/41/59/78) was always a good scalp as were 'Castle' class engines from Stafford Road, Worcester or Landore, the latter recognisable from a distance by their silver buffers. Indeed, almost any 4-6-0 class engine (apart from a 'Manor' class) from any WR shed (except West Wales) was a possibility on a Summer Saturday - though a 'King' class engine from Stafford Road was very exceptional. Most of all, it was the sheer scale of the working which impressed. In busy hours, eight to 10 trains passed in each direction. Unimaginable today.

In contrast, the up platform loop was usually host to the 4.00 pm Exeter Riverside-Taunton freight from around 7.30 pm. It was usually worked either by an unbalanced engine from an earlier working in the day, or by a local '28XX' class engine, such as Nos. 2875, 3834 or 3840. One evening, to our amusement, it appeared behind Exeter's '57XX' class engine No. 3794. How ludicrous this must have seemed, charging up through Burlescombe in the wake of a day-long procession of expresses. Another rare bird one evening, as late as September 1963, was Bristol Barrow Road's 'Jubilee' class engine No. 45690 *Leander* on a down parcels train.

As mentioned earlier, Taunton had a regular quartet of '51XX' class engines until the early 1950s. They were supplemented on the Wellington banking duties by '43XX' class engines, of which Taunton generally had half a dozen, primarily for duties on the Barnstaple branch. Their use on the Minehead branch was unpopular with crews because of the need to use extension pieces on the turntable at Minehead. From 1953, there was a development which upset the notion of a regular quartet. Generally, an additional '51XX' class engine (sometimes two) was allocated to Taunton at the start of summer. It was often the case that the engine(s) transferred away at the end of the summer was not that which arrived at the start. So it was that No. 5157 arrived from Newton Abbot in June 1953 and old faithful No. 4113 departed to the Worcester Division at the end of that summer; No. 4113 survived there until the very end of steam in late 1965.

The start of summer in 1958 saw no less than four '51XX' class engines transferred to Taunton, all from Leamington where they were displaced by the introduction of dmus on the West Midlands suburban service. They were Nos. 4128 (formerly of Birkenhead), 5184, 5185 and 5194. They were very scruffy compared with the regulars (Nos. 4136, 4157, 4159 and 5172, the latter having emerged in lined green livery from Caerphilly works in the previous September). Their arrival coincided with the departure of the last '22XX' class engines at Taunton (Nos. 2212 and 2230), a class associated with Taunton since the delivery of Nos. 2266/67/68 when new in 1930. However, it was all change again at the end of that summer. The last of the original quartet departed. No. 4136 was transferred to Penzance, then leading a nomadic existence being transferred thence to West Wales and finishing its days at Aberdare (working over the Vale of Neath line) in 1964. No. 5172, the old favourite, was condemned only a year after overhaul at Caerphilly. It was one of 16 '51XX' class engines withdrawn in that year. No. 5184 returned to Leamington and No. 5194 moved to Gloucester. To complete the picture, the '22XX' class made a return in the form of No. 2235.

By this date, we were on the threshold of steam's final phase which saw a rapid turnover of engines whose 'tickets' had expired, being replaced by cast-offs from those areas where dieselisation or closures were having their impact. In particular, numerous '61XX' class engines were displaced by dmus in the London Division. The first of these to be allocated to Taunton was No. 6140 in 1959. Others followed. From around 1962, diesels became familiar on banking duties, initially 'D70XX' class engines and then 'D8XX' class engines. The last steam duties were performed by Nos. 4110 and 6148 in 1964, though 'Hall' class engines also appeared in the last year or two. The following tables charts the decline and fall of the '51XX' and '61XX' class engines at Taunton in the last decade of steam:

Year	In	Out (including withdrawn)	Year End Total
1953	5157	4113	4
1954	4176	-	5
1955	4109/50	4109/76	5
1956	4157/59	4150 5157	5
1957	-	4117	4
1958	4128 5184/85/94	4136 5172/84/94	4
1959	4129 6140	4129 6140	4
1960	4117 5198 6155	5185 4159	5
1961	4103/43 6113/48/57	4117/57 5198	7
1962	4110/31 6146	4103/28/31 6146/55/57	4
1963	-	4143 6113/48	1
1964	6148	4110 6148	Nil

Over the years, the bankers performed a yeoman service, unnoticed by the public apart from the residents of Springfield Road and Old Riverside who, in later years, became more vocal in complaining about nocturnal 'crows'. Two incidents reached public attention. One concerned a fatality to one of Wellington's characters - a deaf gentleman who frequented the town on his bicycle with a small terrier dog in the basket over the front wheel. Sadly, all three perished (man, bike and dog) under the wheels of a banker returning to Taunton, when passing over Bradford Crossing one afternoon in November in the mid-1950s. The other incident allegedly concerned No. 4136. A problem with the engine caused the driver to stop and examine it before entering Whiteball tunnel. The train being assisted, of course, was able to continue. There is an important safety feature here. The signalman at Whiteball tunnel signal box must not, in these circumstances, clear the block and accept another train. The rules expressly require the guard (who should have been surprised by the sudden and unexpected loss of sound effects) to replace the tail lamp only in the sight of the signalman and, in addition, to call the signalman's attention to this state of affairs by unspecified gesticulations and articulations. The bank engine traincrew are required to contact the signalman when protecting their engine. In addition, the signalman should be expecting the train to be assisted in rear, having received the supplementary 2-2 bell code from Wellington signal box. Signalmen have to take special care with the working of bank engines, especially when the engine is detained waiting to cross from one running line to another, or waiting acceptance when returning light engine.

Now, it is just a memory. Wellington station closed in October 1964. The yard closed three months earlier. The signal box survived until swept away by the West of England resignalling scheme in 1986. Banking was phased out at the end of the 1960s as a result of much reduced freight activity and the 'single engine' load for the diesel hydraulics being adequate for the remaining traffic. In the 1950s, it was unimaginable that such changes could occur so rapidly and so completely. Such is progress.

Appendix Two

Engine Allocations for August 1962

I have come into the possession of the engine allocation sheet for the late turn at Taunton for Saturday 4th August, 1962. One note on the original sheet reminds me that I was the foreman on duty that day and this was that '73XX' class 2-6-0 No. 7333 was changed over with '43XX' No. 6327 for working the 3.45 pm Taunton to Ilfracombe passenger working. This was a rush job as No. 7333 did not come on shed until 2.00 pm, and when I was handed the allocation sheet No. 6327 caught my eye as I knew that this engine and tender had not had its lower steps cut back to clear the bridge between Barnstaple Junction and Town stations on the Southern Region. All former GWR '43XX', '63XX' and '73XX' Moguls allocated to Taunton for working through to Ilfracombe had a strip approximately 2 in. wide cut from the lower steps for clearance of the girders on this bridge.

A photograph of this bridge has been included courtesy of Peter Triggs.

Below are listed engine numbers and job allocations as taken from a shed engineman's list on Saturday 4th August (late shift 2.00 pm to 10 pm) and a further list for the following day, Sunday 5th August, 1962. This list ensured that engines were turned off shed or stabled in such a manner that no delays were incurred.

Saturday

2.20 pm	Barnstaple Passenger	7337
3.00 pm	Minehead Passenger	4174
3.35 pm	Paddington Passenger	D1002 *(Western Explorer)*
3.37 pm	Minehead Passenger	4128
3.45 pm	Ilfracombe Passenger	6327*
4.30 pm	Wellington and Kensington Milk	4985 *(Allesley Hall)*
4.30 pm	West End Coach Shunter	9670
4.35 pm	Minehead Passenger	4143
4.40 pm	Wellington Banker	4110
4.45 pm	Castle Cary Passenger	6146
5.30 pm	Weston-super-Mare Passenger	4932 *(Hatherton Hall)*
5.50 pm	Yeovil Passenger	6155
5.55 pm	Barnstaple Passenger	7333
6.00 pm	Minehead Passenger	82044
6.20 pm	Exeter Passenger	4904 *(Binnegar Hall)*
7.30 pm	Minehead Passenger	82030
9.15 pm	Minehead Passenger	4103
9.45 pm	Wellington Banker	D70XX (from Bristol)

* On the original sheet this engine changed duties with 7333.

Sunday

1.45 am	Wellington Banker	4103 (after working 9.15 pm Minehead)
4.00 am	Charlton Mackrell Ballast	7326
6.15 am	West Coach Shunter	D4165
8.40 am	Goodrington Passenger	4992 (*Crosby Hall*)
8.50 am	Minehead Passenger	4143
9.00 am	Kingswear Passenger	DXXX (from Bristol)
10.00 am	Charlton Mackrell Relief	9670
11.50 am	Minehead Passenger	4128
1.30 pm	Weston-super-Mare Passenger	4985 (*Allesley Hall*)
2.43 pm	Minehead Passenger	6146

Engines to be stabled inside the shed for 6. 00 am Boiler Washing: 6372, 82030, 3787.

Notes

Some trains were already being worked by diesel locomotives therefore the shed engineman would not know their numbers until they arrived on shed.

No. 4985 *Allesley Hall* would be available to work the 1.30 pm to Weston-super-Mare on Sunday as it would only have worked to Wellington and back to Taunton on Saturday, leaving the milk wagons for picking up by the Paddington Parcels due at Taunton at approximately 9.50 pm.

No. 7337 passes Dulverton signal box with a Barnstaple-Taunton train.   *Exe Rail*

A 1956 Duty Roster

The following sheets are a Duty Roster for Taunton Shed's No. 3 Link for around about 1956. This would be the Winter period as it doesn't include any through workings to Ilfracombe which were covered by this link during the Summer period. These details were kindly provided by Bob Chudleigh.

Notes

Ballast Trains	These were booked entirely on times governed by the requirements of the Engineering Department.
Sunday Rota turns	Footplate crews had to be available to book on duty at any time to cover men who were on leave or off sick, etc. This meant that you had to look at the noticeboard on Saturday night in case you were required.
Depot Relief	This meant that you booked on duty at the engine shed and worked under the instructions of the shed foreman unless you were rostered to cover for leave, sickness etc. You could be required to book on duty hours either side of the stated times to cover for other men.
Control Relief	Book on duty at the engine shed but walk to East Yard and report to and then work under the instructions of Exeter Control Office.

Once you had worked through all 32 turns you started back on Turn 1.

Taunton MPD (83B) Roster for No. 3 Link circa 1956

Turns 1 to 8 Day	Turn 1	Turn 2	Turn 3	Turn 4	Turn 5	Turn 6	Turn 7	Turn 8
Sunday	Rota		12.30 pm Control Relief		Off		2nd Ballast	
Monday	4.35 pm Tiverton Jn Goods	5.40 am Yeovil Goods	2.00 pm Control Relief	2.00 am Depot Relief	Rest Day Off	5.30 am Barnstaple Goods	3.25 pm N. Abbot Goods	6.52 am Yeovil Passenger
Tuesday	4.35 pm Tiverton Jn Goods	5.40 am Yeovil Goods	2.00 pm Control Relief	2.00 am Depot Relief	11.15 pm N. Abbot Goods	5.30 am Barnstaple Goods	3.25 pm N. Abbot Goods	6.52 am Yeovil Passenger
Wednesday	Rest Day Off	5.40 am Yeovil Goods	2.00 pm Control Relief	2.00 am Depot Relief	11.15 pm N. Abbot Goods	5.30 am Barnstaple Goods	3.25 pm N. Abbot Goods	6.52 am Yeovil Passenger
Thursday	4.35 pm Tiverton Jn Goods	5.40 am Yeovil Goods	2.00 pm Control Relief	2.00 am Depot Relief	11.15 pm N. Abbot Goods	5.30 am Barnstaple Goods	Rest Day Off	6.52 am Yeovil Passenger
Friday	4.35 pm Tiverton Jn Goods	5.40 am Yeovil Goods	2.00 pm Control Relief	2.00 am Depot Relief	11.15 pm N. Abbot Goods	5.30 am Barnstaple Goods	3.25 pm N. Abbot Goods	6.52 am Yeovil Passenger
Saturday	4.35 pm Tiverton Jn Goods	5.40 am Yeovil Goods	2.00 pm Control Relief	Rest Day Off	11.15 pm N. Abbot Goods	5.30 am Barnstaple Goods	3.25 pm N. Abbot Goods	6.52 am Yeovil Passenger

Taunton MPD (83B) Roster for No. 3 Link circa 1956 (continued)

Turns 9 to 16

Day	Turn 9	Turn 10	Turn 11	Turn 12	Turn 13	Turn 14	Turn 15	Turn 16
Sunday	10.00 pm Control Relief		12.30 pm Control Relief		3rd Ballast Relief		2.00 pm Control Relief	
Monday	8.00 pm Control Relief	7.30 am Depot Relief	6.00 pm Depot Relief	10.40 am Highbridge Goods	9.00 pm Depot Relief	12.00 noon Depot Relief	2.30 pm Depot Relief	3.00 am Depot Relief
Tuesday	6.00 pm Depot Relief	7.30 am Depot Relief	Rest Day Off	10.40 am Highbridge Goods	Rest Day Off	12.00 noon Depot Relief	2.30 pm Depot Relief	3.00 am Depot Relief
Wednesday	5.00 pm Barnstaple Passenger	7.30 am Depot Relief	6.00 pm Depot Relief	10.40 am Highbridge Goods	9.00 pm Depot Relief	12.00 noon Depot Relief	2.30 pm Depot Relief	3.00 am Depot Relief
Thursday	3.25 pm N. Abbot Goods	7.30 am Depot Relief	6.00 pm Depot Relief	10.40 am Highbridge Goods	9.00 pm Depot Relief	12.00 noon Depot Relief	2.30 pm Depot Relief	3.00 am Depot Relief
Friday	Rest Day Off	7.30 am Depot Relief	6.00 pm Depot Relief	10.40 am Highbridge Goods	9.00 pm Depot Relief	12.00 noon Depot Relief	2.30 pm Depot Relief	3.00 am Depot Relief
Saturday	6.35 am Exeter Goods	7.30 am Depot Relief	6.00 pm Depot Relief	10.40 am Highbridge Goods	9.00 pm Depot Relief	12.00 noon Depot Relief	2.30 pm Depot Relief	Rest Day Off

Turns 17 to 24

Day	Turn 17	Turn 18	Turn 19	Turn 20	Turn 21	Turn 22	Turn 23	Turn 24
Sunday	Off		9.30 pm Control Relief		10.30 am Control Relief		Rota	
Monday	Rest Day Off	10.00 am Depot Relief	10.00 pm Control Relief	4.00 am Depot Relief	10.00 pm Depot Relief	6.00 am Control Relief	8.25 pm Bristol Goods	8.00 am Depot Relief
Tuesday	10.33 pm Westbury Goods	10.00 am Depot Relief	10.00 pm Control Relief	4.00 am Depot Relief	9.00 pm Depot Relief	6.00 am Control Relief	8.25 pm Bristol Goods	8.00 am Depot Relief
Wednesday	10.33 pm Westbury Goods	10.00 am Depot Relief	10.00 pm Control Relief	4.00 am Depot Relief	8.25 pm Bristol Goods	6.00 am Control Relief	Rest Day Off	8.00 am Depot Relief
Thursday	10.33 pm Westbury Goods	10.00 am Depot Relief	10.00 pm Control Relief	4.00 am Depot Relief	Rest Day Off	6.00 am Control Relief	8.25 pm Bristol Goods	8.00 am Depot Relief
Friday	10.33 pm Westbury Goods	10.00 am Depot Relief	10.00 pm Control Relief	Rest Day Off	4.00 am Depot Relief	6.00 am Control Relief	8.25 pm Bristol Goods	8.00 am Depot Relief
Saturday	10.33 pm Westbury Goods	10.00 am Depot Relief	10.00 pm Control Relief	4.00 am Depot Relief	8.00 am Depot Relief	6.00 am Control Relief	8.25 pm Bristol Goods	8.00 am Depot Relief

Taunton MPD (83B) Roster for No. 3 Link circa 1956 (continued)

Turns 25 to 32

Day	Turn 25	Turn 26	Turn 27	Turn 28	Turn 29	Turn 30	Turn 31	Turn 32
Sunday	7.30 am Control Relief		Off		1st Ballast Relief		Rota	12.45 am Control Relief
Monday	6.50 pm N. Abbot Goods	6.00 am Depot Relief	Rest Day Off	9.40 am N. Abbot Goods	5.00 pm Barnstaple Passenger	6.55 am S. Molton Goods	6.15 pm Barnstaple Passenger	2.28 pm N. Abbot Goods
Tuesday	6.50 pm N. Abbot Goods	6.35 am Exeter Goods	6.15 pm Barnstaple Passenger	9.40 am N. Abbot Goods	5.00 pm Barnstaple Passenger	6.55 am S. Molton Goods	4.00 pm Depot Relief	2.28 pm N. Abbot Goods
Wednesday	6.50 pm N. Abbot Goods	6.35 am Exeter Goods	6.15 pm Barnstaple Passenger	9.40 am N. Abbot Goods	Rest Day Off	6.55 am S. Molton Goods	4.35 pm Tiverton Jn Goods	2.28 pm N. Abbot Goods
Thursday	6.50 pm N. Abbot Goods	6.35 am Exeter Goods	6.15 pm Barnstaple Passenger	9.40 am N. Abbot Goods	5.00 pm Barnstaple Passenger	6.55 am S. Molton Goods	Rest Day Off	2.28 pm N. Abbot Goods
Friday	6.50 pm N. Abbot Goods	6.35 am Exeter Goods	6.15 pm Barnstaple Passenger	9.40 am N. Abbot Goods	5.00 pm Barnstaple Passenger	6.55 am S. Molton Goods	5.00 am Depot Relief	2.28 pm N. Abbot Goods
Saturday	6.50 pm N. Abbot Goods	Rest Day Off	6.15 pm Barnstaple Passenger	9.40 am N. Abbot Goods	4.35 pm Barnstaple Passenger	6.55 am S. Molton Goods	2.00 am Depot Relief	2.28 pm N. Abbot Goods

A Mogul approaches Barnstaple (Victoria Road) with a train from Taunton on 28th September, 1956. *H.C. Casserley*